Jesus - My Song of Songs

Our Dance within the Song
Henri Rising

DEDICATION

I owe a great thanks to my husband David and my family for always believing in me.   Also to Phil & Jan Bonner, Larry & Carole Terherst, and Darrel & Darlene Watson for sowing into my life.   I cannot forget Judy Bailey for continually giving me the motivation to keep going and Judy Anderson for editing the entire book.

You have learned to recognize and understand My voice. I am calling you into a deeper fellowship. I will not push My desires on you. You must come freely, on your own. All preconceived ideas must be left behind. Until now you have only thought of My glory and power. I am crucified. I must have crucified followers. Come in deeper. I wish to take My bride into the depth and breadth of My sufferings & death. Many of you say, "Isn't it enough that I have put off my old nature and way of life?" I say, Come in deeper, bare your feet! Without shoes, your feet become more sensitive. Every pebble, every thorn, every rock can be felt. Things you did not feel before, you will now feel. You will share in My sufferings. You will understand how My Spirit responds to sin. You will feel My heartbreak over the rebellion of man and My hurt in being rejected by My creation whom I love. I want you to feel the depths of My love. My Spirit will flow through you so fully that the world will attack, not you, but My Spirit within you. You will become jealous on My behalf to see My Holiness go forth on the earth. I say, Come deeper into My fire, into My death. Many of you however, through fear, will shrink back from My call. Fear of consequences, fear of losing present blessings, fear of the unknown, fear of being deprived of familiar comforts, and indefinable fear of the reality of suffering. You must come into My death before My resurrection life can be manifested in you. Step into My death and emerge with the fullness of My life!

If you study the Song of Songs, you will see that the bride is invited into the Lord's death. Then when she emerges in the end as a mature bride she is sent out into the vineyards. The Lord is coming back for his bride....the mature bride. Certain things, although they seem unpleasant...must be...to obtain the maturity the Lord seeks. The only true way to understand total rejection is to live through it. Trust in the Lord, stand strong and keep walking forward. Once you understand the rejection Jesus felt, you will be able to feel His heart in a deeper measure. Then your hunger for the lost to come to the Lord will increase like never before.

The most important thing to remember about the Song is that it is a story about you! The word is living and current for today. This is not so much about the symbolism in the story but the way the story lives in my life. I only hope by reading this, you too, will see it come alive in your life.

Henri Rising

Jesus – My Song of Songs
Our Dance within the Song

Chapter 1
Finding Love and the Chambers

Dance -A rhythmic and patterned succession of movements, commonly to music.

The steps of a good man are ordered by the LORD, And He delights in his way.   Psalm 37:23

I believe that inside of every heart is a dance, an ordered set of steps that will lead us directly to our Lord, King and Bridegroom. The problem is that we seek and sometimes settle for dancing with things of this world. The satisfaction is not found and we continue trying different partners of the world when our true partner is found in the Spirit. Understanding the Song of Songs will help you find the perfect partner.

I saw a little girl standing before Jesus.
He held out His hand and said,
"Will you dance with Me?"
She happily jumped up and did what she had always done.....
She stood on His feet and took His hand ready for the dance.
He looked at her and said,
"No, now is the time for you to stand on the ground.
Time to stand on what I have taught you....
But you must remember,
It is I who asked you to dance.
It is I who leads the dance.
If you follow my lead…
No toes will be stepped on…
No steps will be missed.
The dance will flow freely only
If you follow My lead!"

The song of songs, which is Solomon's (1:1)

This is a love song of heaven. This is a cry of a bride who longs for a fullness of transformation by her Lord. Solomon wrote 1,000 songs (1 Kings 4:30) of which the Song of Songs was the best of the best. I personally cannot even imagine writing one song let alone over one thousand. How full his heart must have been to have it pour out in song. The name Solomon means 'peaceful' or 'prince of peace'. Solomon's reign of peace only foreshadowed the reign of the one and only Prince of Peace. This is a book of the heart, a book for those seeking a deeper spiritual communion with God. It is a pathway to destiny and peace.

I began my dance in 1993. The Holy Ghost was moving in the small church my husband and I had just started attending. It was an incredible time of healing in my life. Each time I came into the sanctuary, the Lord touched me deeply, until I was so drawn in by his touch, I gave him my heart. I came from a background of abuse - physical, sexual & emotional. I suffered a lot of rejection in my life. I was very withdrawn from the world and did not talk much with people. I had too much fear deep inside me. I had very little trust for anyone or anything and had no peace at all. I could not believe anything I heard about love and peace could ever be for me. In my mind I was worthless. This is a story of how God changed me.

Jesus loves you
This I know because
My bible tells me so
Jesus loves me
This I know because
He deeply touched my soul.

One day as I lay on the floor of this little church in God's presence, allowing the Lord to wash away a life time of hurt, I heard a thought, a sound come into my mind saying softly… "You will find the love you seek in the Song of Songs". I was not even sure where that was in the bible but I got up and opened up the book. At that point, I began to walk a pathway to find what I could not understand – love.

Let him kiss me with the kisses of his mouth: for thy love is better than wine. (1:2)
When the bride is near the Lord, she is longing to have greater access to him. She does not call the one she is longing for by name. She only describes him as her Beloved or the One whom her soul loves. She speaks of him as if there is no other but him on the earth. I longed to be so close to the bridegroom that my whole thought & heart would be only of Him. I saw people deeply in love that would unconsciously just assume that everyone around them also saw the beauty and wonderful qualities of the one they loved. When I was younger I read romance stories of perfect romances. I had experienced no real love growing up. I can't even remember my mother ever hugging or kissing me. The only father figures in my life definitely did not line up with any of those stories. I wanted to experience, to understand what this love was all about. It was like there was a huge hole inside of me and until now, nothing I could find would fill it or even really had a hope to fill it up. Up to this moment, I had made it a point in my life to numb everything with drugs. It was my way of coping with the hole, the emptiness. I just knew that if I could somehow understand this love that I would find fulfillment, something to keep on living for. The struggle to understand was not easy and I can honestly say that there were many times I almost gave in and at times did give into the former ways of dealing with life. Each time my Savior, my King, my Lover would come to my rescue.

I remember getting up off the floor and reading the first chapter of the Song and really not understanding what I was reading. I looked around and one of the elders was near. I took my bible to him and asked, "What do you think this means?" I will never forget his answer. You will have to understand that he knew that I was very new in the Lord and obviously had some issues to deal with. Perhaps he was surprised that I actually approached him alone and talked. He replied, "What are you doing in that book? You need to begin in the gospels or Ephesians."

The "pre-Jesus" me would have never looked at the Song of Songs ever again. Something happens when the Lord touches you so deeply, you believe Him! I just knew I heard something extraordinary for my life as I was on the floor, something just for me. I did read Ephesians and the gospels but my reading and my heart always headed for the Song of Songs first. Extraordinary means beyond the common order or method; exceeding the common degree, measure, or condition; remarkable; employed for a special service; as an ambassador. The hunt for the meaning, the secret contained there just seemed to consume me.

At this point in my life, I had still been slipping away to get high while no one was looking. I soon found myself forgetting about the physical high and was consumed with the spiritual high I was getting in God's presence and learning to understand His love.

I wish I could say that letting go of my old self was easy. I am not there but I am so much closer than I was before. It is a long but very worthwhile journey. I never understood that you could really enjoy waking up and just living the day ahead of you.

I wondered, "How He could kiss me with the kisses of His mouth? Did the Lord get that close? What would that be like?" In a way, I look back and think, how could I have been so touched by God and still so unsure of His love?

In Numbers 12:6-8 the Lord spoke to Miriam and Aaron when they were opposing Moses.

Then He said, "Hear now My words: If there is a prophet among you, I, the LORD, make Myself known to him in a vision; I speak to him in a dream. Not so with My servant Moses; He [is] faithful in all My house. I speak with him face to face, Even plainly, and not in dark sayings; And he sees the form of the LORD. Why then were you not afraid To speak against My servant Moses?"

The key words here are face to face. In the Hebrew, this verse reads mouth to mouth. Sounded like a kiss to me. Kiss actually means to put together, to gently touch, to equip. This was exactly what I needed and longed for. This sounded better than any wine, any drug and better than anything I could imagine. It was wonderful and yet so frightening. The most tender, gentle expression of love that we can know is a kiss, it is something we all should understand. My heart began to cry out, "Let Him kiss me!"

Coming from a background of abuse, this cry surprised me. I had always run from any type of intimacy unless I was high on some drug. I had to let the Lord cleanse my mind of my preconceived ideas of a kiss. The past had taught me that kisses were not good things. Here was something I had always run from (unless I was high) and all of the sudden, I was crying out for it.

His love began to consume me. I could hardly walk into the church and the Spirit would hit me and I would find myself on the floor in His presence once again. All of the sudden, I understood the meaning of a kiss. It really was a very tender, gentle expression of love. The world and the enemy had given me damaged perspective of love. "Let Him kiss me with the kisses of His mouth!"

His love here meant to me the continual proofs and tokens of His love. Never have grown up surrounded by love, it seemed like I continually needed to see, to feel His love to keep on believing this love was for me. The wine symbolized all the good and desirable things of the world. (note: all desirable things are not necessarily good.) I was beginning to believe that His love was better than all the walls of protection I had built. It seemed more and more like it would be a good idea to come out from those walls to obtain this love.

Because of the savour of thy good ointments thy name is as ointment poured forth, therefore do the virgins love thee (1:3)
I pondered on what exactly is a pleasing fragrance? I think this is different to each of us, a very individual sense. What is pleasing to my husband is not so pleasing to me. He loves scented candles, but they tend to give me sinus headaches. I like the scent of the candles but I just know the after effects are not always pleasant for me, so I avoid them. Could this be true in the Spiritual also?
I think the sense of smell has an association with physical experiences. I have a friend who loves the smell of cattle manure. She grew up on a ranch and it brings back fond memories, so it is a pleasant smell to her. In the temple the High Priest ministered to the Lord. They used a perfume that was only made for that purpose. No man could use it upon his flesh. It was reserved exclusively for ministering to God.

As the High Priest ministered to God and burned the oils, he was so close, the perfumes could not help but to envelope him and the clothing he wore. I can only imagine the sweet smell that remained on them. As the priest left the Holy of Holies and passed among the people of Israel, the sweet smell must have been very noticeable to all who were close. So we should be to God's people, so sweet smelling from the scent of His oil, which has enveloped us as we minister to our King that we give off the fragrance of His character as we live our lives.

I think many times the things happening around us; distract us from "smelling" the sweetness of His character which is being poured out on us through the name of Jesus. In the physical we avoid things that could possibly cause us pain. In the presence of God's character we see our own flaws. I can't lie to you and say letting the Lord change those flaws is always easy. It takes some participation on your behalf.

Have you ever just been drawn into a room, a place just by the fragrance emitting from it? This sweetest aroma to me is the aroma of the character of Jesus within a room. The name Christ means, "The Anointed One". You have to get close enough to smell the perfume, to let the aroma draw you in. Once you smell the sweetness of His pure love and Holiness, His submission to His father's will, His purity and longsuffering, you realize it is a smell like no other. It draws you in but also makes you realize that your flesh 'stinks' with its lack of pure love, disobedience and our short suffering for others. Then His smell overpowers you with the sweet perfume of forgiveness and great patience. When you think about smells, it is that which smells sweetest to you that can draw you in. The sweet smell of Jesus is the opposite of the smell of our weakest places. When our alabaster box, Jesus, was broken on the cross, His sweet fragrance flowed out filling heaven and earth. Heaven's perfume came to earth for all of us to freely partake of.

I love the old saying, "Take time to smell the roses." Take time out of your busy life to smell the sweetest One, that is and will ever be. By laying me 'flat out' on the floor, the Lord not only got rid of any pride and fears of being vulnerable, he taught me to take the time to quiet myself and enjoy the sweetness of his fragrance.

This was not an instantly learned lesson for me; it progressed over a period of 5 years. My friends use to tease me about '*my spot*' on the floor. I didn't care; the perfume was drawing me in, closer to Him. It was an attraction that no drug ever had.

Eph 5:1-2 Therefore be imitators of God as dear children. And walk in love, as Christ also has loved us and given Himself for us, an offering and a sacrifice to God for a sweet-smelling aroma.

Draw me, we will run after thee: the king hath brought me into his chambers: we will be glad and rejoice in thee, we will remember thy love more than wine: the upright love thee. (1:4)
All of the sudden I could smell His wonderful fragrance. I began to not only to be drawn into it but realized that I was calling out "draw me". I wanted more, it was becoming as an addiction, this love offered freely to me. I knew I could not do this on my own; I needed Him to draw me. He was the only one who could accomplish this in my life.

Jer 31:3 The Lord has appeared of old to me, saying: "Yes, I have loved you with an everlasting love; Therefore with loving kindness I have drawn you."

In an instant it seemed like my heart sprang up out of me and I desired to rise up and run as I had never done before. The more I began to rise up; the more it became a reality to me that I was helpless to run without His drawing. Somehow I knew this drawing would include understanding and loving the Father also.

John 6:44 No one can come to Me unless the Father who sent Me draws him; and I will raise him up at the last day.

I realized that every person who makes up the bride of Christ must have a personal dealing, drawing in his or her lives, a personal working in the individual soul. We are in the midst of others who are running, yet running a personal path. I saw many who would quit with the first stone they stepped on or the first sign of being tired.

All I could do was to cry out more fervently, "Draw me Lord and I WILL run after you!" Yes, I was growing tired but I was hearing a call to rest in His arms. The closer I got, the greater the fragrance became and the greater the drawing. I wanted to hear His voice whether it was pleasant to my ears or reproof. It didn't matter what He was saying to me, it was the most wonderful thing I had ever heard.

Psalm 63:8 My soul follows close behind You; Your right hand upholds me.

This verse literally means that my soul runs clinging to you. It didn't matter what He said to me or asked me to do, I knew somehow He would see me through it. I began to run faster and faster, clinging to Him.

Duet 4:29 "But from there you will seek the LORD your God, and you will find Him if you seek Him with all your heart and with all your soul."

I wanted to never forget what a treasure there was in this great hunger and thirst I was feeling. What I was feeling was all because of Him for He was the one putting this desire deep within me. This was so different from the physical. As a child when I went hungry and thirsty, I found no delight in it. I only knew that no one cared about the situation but now it was so different. It has become a great delight to hunger and be filled but only to hunger again. It seemed with each hunger pang, the greater the abandonment to Him. I was running after Him crying, "Make me hunger and thirst!"

It was like being in the mall and walking past the food court and suddenly becoming really hungry. I think it is a place of great favor to feel that hunger, that drawing from the Lord, which leads to continual abandonment. I was beginning to believe that as long as I ran faster and faster, not letting go of Him, that he would see me through those hard places, catch me as I stumbled and help me to keep going forward as I headed down my path.

It was so amazing to me that this path ran into His chambers, that secret place we were beginning to share together. What was even more amazing was the fact the there was no way I could prepare myself for this moment. He simply loved me, in the midst of all my sin, and had brought me into this wonderful place. No drug could ever do this for me. There was no great test to prove myself worthy or no work I could do to get here, he just drew me to Him and brought me in.

Notice that word chambers is not singular but plural. With each step I took, each chamber, I knew there was another to be drawn into. This is a process that is ongoing until we meet our Bridegroom face to face in heaven. To me personally, I could see the first chamber as being brought into salvation. I didn't think any place could be or feel as wonderful as this.

Then I felt the drawing again, so I began to seek with all my heart. I knew He was drawing me into a new place, a new chamber. As I entered this new chamber I became baptized in the Holy Spirit. Could anything be better than this?

Over the years I have entered many chambers with Him. Notice I said with Him, you couldn't do it on your own. Some chambers I visit over and over. If I were to put names to them I would label them love, peace, mercy, grace, humility, healing, faith, and victory. It is a path leading from glory to glory. Each is different to enter for me. The door to humility seemed so small; I had to get down on my knees to crawl through it. As I got down on my knees, I even wondered if it would be worth all this effort, even though I knew it would be. Funny, our flesh always wants the easy way to enter. What a wonderful place, I entered to find myself directly at the feet of Jesus. The chamber of healing had a wide open door, yet to me it seemed so scary to enter into. Fear and doubt had to leave as I entered. As I entered each chamber, I got a clearer revelation of my Lord. I entered into experiences that I knew a person could never experience without walking through the door.

Even though He brought me into each chamber and was with me, I knew this was not always an easy place to be. He was there for me always, something I had never experienced in my life. For a time I rejoiced in what he was doing in my life, seeking those experiences.

Then I began to see the truth. These experiences were wonderful but the more I entered in, the more I began to rejoice in Him not the experiences. You have to see that rejoicing in experiences is very conditional.

As my love for Him began to grow, it did not matter what He did or did not do, it's all about who He is! Gladness is an inward joy and satisfaction; rejoicing is an outward condition of an inward condition. The memory of any satisfaction I thought I got from drugs seemed to fade. It could not compare to this. It just seemed right to love someone so incredibly wonderful.

Chapter 2
Finding Myself & the Great Shepherd

I am black, but comely, O ye daughters of Jerusalem, as the tents of Kedar, as the curtains of Solomon.
Look not upon me, because I am black, because the sun hath looked upon me: my mother's children were angry with me; they made me the keeper of the vineyards; but mine own vineyard have I not kept. (1:5-6)
I knew I was a sinner. Even though these wonderful things were happening in my life, I continued to sin. I tried but failed so many times and yet I knew that I was somehow a pleasing sight to my Lord. My seeking and sometimes failing still pleased him. I kept seeing my sin because I had seen His beauty; it had opened my eyes to my blackness. It was a clearness I had never experienced before. I thought that everyone else could also see how unfit I was to stand within the King's presence. I felt all that brokenness left by the world and the darkness on me from my sin was in full view. The black tents of Kedar were tents covered in black goatskins to keep the sun out. What a contrast to the white tents of Solomon. I was seeing myself as black but yet beginning to see how he had made me white. It was confusing.

Each person who draws closer to the Lord soon begins to feel his or her unworthiness. I was being drawn despite my feelings. I decided to somehow get past that feeling of wanting to hide from the others in the church. I needed get past that fleshly feeling of embarrassment of my great need.
I want you to think of the situation I was facing. Every time I would come forward at church and raised my hands, the Spirit would fall upon me and I would find myself on the floor in His presence for hours.

I needed to know, because of the great rejection I had experienced in my life, that each time I came to the Lord, he would be there. He did not fail me but I knew the people could not help but watch because it was so incredible. From the moment I stood up, I could see people watching me. I did not want to be the center of attention. Growing up, if you caught the attention of the adults around you, it usually meant trouble and pain. I had always tried to be as invisible as possible and now this wonderful marvelous drawing was taking me into a place in the physical that caused great anxiety in my soul. Yet the feeling of His presence kept overshadowing my fears.

If I could just muster up enough courage to make to the front and raise my hands, I knew it would be ok. Soon it began to seem like every one of the many evangelists that came to our church called me out for a word. I found myself again in the spotlight, yet I needed to know what God had for me. I did not want others to be distracted from the beauty of God by my blackness which I felt was fully exposed for all to see. There was balance I needed to find.

I needed to find the place where I could behold the beauty of God and know he is was my everything; yet still is able to see those dark areas in my life that I needed to work on without great shame. I needed to work on my own vineyards, yet keep sight of the things the Lord would have me do for him. Anyone who thinks the Lord cannot use them until they 'clean up' is sadly mistaken. God just wants us to be willing and obedient.

I love the flowerbeds at my house. I know that even though my husband designed them to be as maintenance free as possible they still require constant care. Weeds need to be pulled, watering must be regular and spent flowers need to be clipped. So it is the same with our souls. You cannot water others if you do not water yourself. If you attempt this, you will soon become very dry.

Tell me, O thou whom my soul loveth, where thou feedest, where thou makest thy flock to rest at noon: for why should I be as one that turneth aside by the flocks of thy companions? If thou know not, O thou fairest among women, go thy way forth by the footsteps of the flock, and feed thy kids beside the shepherds' tents. (1:7-8)
With a great, deep intensity I began to find my prayers began to call out to the Lord asking to show me the place where I could find Him. I had felt His drawing, entered chambers with Him but I was feeling the need for a deeper meeting place with Him. I did not even know if that was possible. I wanted all the food He had for me, so I had this great desire to go to the source. "Where do you feed your flocks?"

As a child, living in a very dysfunctional atmosphere, I would look at the other children at school and I just wanted to be normal and belong to a normal family. One day the Lord asked me, "What do you think is normal?" I realized that there really is no 'normal'. Normal is simply being average. It also changes with each family, each country and place. It's the average of where you are. I did not any longer wish to be 'normal', for I knew I was created for something different...a unique purpose.

"Why should I be like everyone else who comes to that average place to feed, who are comfortable in the rest there and never truly revealing their inner heart?" I asked.

I did not want to be one who followed the companions of the Lord, I wanted to follow the Lord himself. I was looking for a pathway that leads to spiritual maturity. Somehow I knew as I revealed myself to Him, with my heart unveiled I would begin to see a greater revelation of the One I was seeking. I could see the 'companions' around me knew the Lord and I also wanted to know Him better also.

I was feeling that I still had a veil that covered my face and that kept me from seeing knowing the Lord more intimately. Then I heard him tenderly, sweetly drawing me closer. It was as if He were saying, "If you don't understand yet, follow the footsteps of those who have found me until you can remove your veil and see Me clearly for yourself." At first I was a little offended by this statement, and then I thought about His heart that only wanted the best for me. Somehow I also knew through this following I would not only learn obedience but some humility also.

I have compared thee, O my love, to a company of horses in Pharaoh's chariots. (1:9)
Hearing God speak into your life is so uplifting because He sees your heart, as you will be and not what you are or you perceive yourself to be. The pharaoh's horses were the finest in the land, famous for their beauty and speed. These horses were highly valued because they were the most surefooted and swiftest of all. They could go easily over the hills and down into the valleys, bypass obstacles. In battle, they obeyed even in the face of death. They drew the chariots with all the splendor and glory of the king.

As he spoke this to my heart, I was in awe to know that he already saw me running in His splendor and glory, passing those that I had been following. I felt so unworthy of His assessment of me.

He reminded me of Gideon who was hiding in the winepress in fear of the enemy. The angel said to Gideon, "Jehovah is with thee, thou mighty man of valor." It was obvious that there was not much in Gideon to make him a mighty man of valor at that moment. When the Lord is with you, the possibilities in your life are endless. The Lord led him until his gentleness made him great and he really did become a mighty man of valor. Wow, could it be possible that he could do the same for me? Could I become surefooted? It seems like I stumble so much and the hills are so hard to climb. Many times I just want to hide from the enemy.

Thy cheeks are comely with rows of jewels, thy neck with chains of gold. (1:10)
The women of the East would decorate their cheeks with jewels. It would look as if their faces were framed in jewels. I believe the jewels here are God's character and grace. It was my King speaking to me saying, "You see yourself as unworthy and burnt by the sun, I see you as the beauty of my reflection." I see you covered in the beauty of My character and grace. Your will (symbolized by the neck) is covered with chains of my glory." I just could not see myself that way, so I had no choice but to trust Him. Somehow I would grow into that picture. I knew this was so because My Lord had told me so. Do you believe that is how the Lord sees you?

Immediately the boy's father exclaimed, "I do believe; help me overcome my unbelief!" Mark 9:24

We will make thee borders of gold with studs of silver. (1:11)
Most people interpret this verse as sung by the Daughters of Jerusalem but I am not so sure. To me, it was showing me that the Father, Son and Holy Spirit were joining together to crown me in their beauty.

This just enforced the great need in me to get to know all three. Jesus was easy, but learning to know the Father would be a process for me. My perception of a loving father did not exist. I was unsure of my relationship with the Holy Spirit because at this point I couldn't distinguish between my flesh and the Holy Spirit. This path seemed so impossible yet still attainable and this just did not make sense to me.

The gold that was to be my covering would be the divine nature of Jesus Christ; this seemed to imply that there would be a lot of refining in this process. Ornaments in the original Hebrew meant something like a braided crown.

The ransomed of the Lord will return. They will enter Zion with singing; everlasting joy will crown their heads. Gladness and joy will overtake them, and sorrow and sighing will flee away. Isaiah 51:11

This braided crown will have studs of silver. Silver represents atonement. This crown is given to me and you, the bride, despite what others would think. Only Jesus would come to earth as a man to die so that His bride would be redeemed. He places his divine nature upon our heads, our sinful nature, our flesh but it has studs that shine with the atoning work of Christ in our lives.

I am coming soon. Hold on to what you have, so that no one will take your crown. Rev 3:11

I knew I still had this 'victim' mentality and often allowed people to walk all over me. I didn't know how to stand up for myself and just say no. How could all this be for me? Then God gave me a dream.

My husband had purchased this cute little puppy for me for Valentine's Day. I had a great love for this puppy. I called her Calley Sue. In my dream a knock came to the door and I answered it, holding Calley Sue in my arms. A man stood there and simply stated, "I have come to take Calley Sue". I just stood there and watched in horror and he reached over and took her from my arms. Then a resounding voice said, "Why do you always allow others to take what is precious to you?"

God speaks to each of us in a way so personal to bring about understanding. I began to see the preciousness of this gift He was giving to me and I had to somehow learn not to let others take it away from me.

While the king sitteth at his table, my spikenard sendeth forth the smell thereof. (1:12)
The Lord had given me direction on how to find Him and had upheld me while I stumbled and searched for Him. As He had asked of me, I followed the companions in obedience until I found myself beside His tents and there was my king at HIS table. Notice that he did not meet me at my table but brought me through obedience to His table.

This was a table spread before me in green pastures. My heart was overflowing with His loving kindness, grace and mercy. I had entered a place of communion with Him that was so deep and intimate; it surpassed anything I had known. This place, in His presence, was not only feeding me but was giving me a rest in my spirit that I had never felt before. This was way beyond my comprehension. I was beginning to understand the verse in John 4:34 where Jesus said, "My food is to do the will of Him who sent me and to finish His work".

He had become the King of my life and sitting at His table in such close intimacy only made me long to do His will to a greater degree than before. As I began to feed off this table He had set before me, my life began to give off a sweet smell to God and others around me.

It is interesting the smell here is of Spikenard. It is a useful and valuable plant. Spikenard rhizomes (underground stems) can be crushed and distilled into an intensely aromatic amber-colored essential oil, which is very thick in consistency. It is commonly called nard oil and is used as a perfume, incense, a sedative, and an herbal medicine said to fight insomnia, birth difficulties, and other minor ailments. Emotionally this oil is reserved for deep seated grief or old pain. It is used in palliative care to help ease the transition from life to death.

Wow! Can you look at this description of Spikenard infused into the spiritual side of my life and see what was happening deep inside me as I partook in intimacy at this level with the King? I was receiving a mighty healing in my life just by finding and spending time with my King. It probably was a good thing not to be able to discern the smell of this spikenard at that time. I would have not been fond of the transition from life to death. I would have not understood that the life of the flesh had to die for me to fully live in Him.

For if you live according to the flesh you will die; but if by the Spirit you put to death the deeds of the body, you will live. Romans 8:13

A bundle of myrrh is my wellbeloved unto me; he shall lie all night betwixt my breasts. (1:13)
After feeling God's presence each time I lifted my hands to him, it became time for me to realize that He was my bundle of myrrh.

Myrrh also has very interesting properties. It is an embalming spice and used in the embalming of Jesus. It keeps things from corrupting, smelling and rotting. It is also good to take away wrinkles from the face making the skin shining and smooth. Myrrh has a wonderful healing quality and is used to dress wounds. It also has a perfuming quality, the first and main ingredient in the holy anointing oil used in the tabernacle. In the eastern countries, women use fragrance freely, even placing little aromatic herbs or oils in a little bag, which is concealed next to their breasts. This custom puts off a fragrant aroma for all that are near.

Night in the Song of Solomon seems to symbolize times that the Bridegroom is not near. My King was becoming my secret perfume, which filled my heart. It seemed like the times that I felt He was not close to me that this perfume began to fill my heart. Sweet is the smell of His presence within my heart.
Myrrh is not only sweet but also bitter and symbolizes suffering. I was beginning to see beyond my need and to share in His sufferings. This bitterness that I was partaking of somehow was putting off a sweet smell to others around me. Was I willing to suffer the loss of all the things that I had held on to so tightly to for so long, just to know Him at a greater level? Only as myrrh is crushed and pierced, does it give off its sweet fragrance. There were so many things in my life that still need to be crushed and pierced for me to give off that sweet smell in a greater measure. I could not still stay in control of my heart, no matter what pain it caused me. I had to latch on to the promises in the word.

For His anger is but for a moment, His favor is for life; Weeping may endure for a night, But joy comes in the morning.   Psalm 30:5

How many times would I have to cry out, "Why have you forsaken me?" Then I would realize that the LORD is near to those who have a broken heart, And saves such as have a contrite spirit. Psalm 34:18

Peace I leave with you, My peace I give to you; not as the world gives do I give to you. Let not your heart be troubled, neither let it be afraid. John 14:27

I would remember reading that Jesus had said, "I will never leave you nor forsake you." It was just so incredibly hard at times to let go of those old hurts. Sometimes I just felt so alone. There is a time when you have to grow beyond the physical experience and begin to believe in your heart that He is always there for you. God is so patient with us. One night as I was hitting one of my low spots and really struggling with just living each moment, my Savior came to me. His presence manifest while I lay on my bed.

All of the sudden I could feel a wind. It's blowing gently on my face. Then I heard these words speaking softly into my heart… "Can you hear it? Can you feel it? I am here. Listen. Listen. Feel My presence. Do you hear Me calling? My burden is so light. Why do you carry so much? I am willing to take it all. Can you not see that I am here? Embrace Me for none of those things can stay in My presence. Do you not know that just as much as you need Me, that I long for you? My heart is lovesick for your closeness. We belong together always." (I feel the wind, I hear the wind) "Listen…Listen…I am here. Come, for I am here. I long for you. Come."

Needless to say I made it to work the next day. As I worked my way through the day, I received an email from my Pastor concerned about what was going on in my life. As he wrote, suddenly he began to speak a word from the Lord. I never told him about the encounter I had the night before.

This is what the Lord said through my pastor .... "Know that you are mine. I have caught you out of great destruction, great destruction. I am holding you close in My arms. I have not let you down from the day I caught you when you were falling. You have grown use to My touch; you have become accustomed to the feel of My arms around you. You have become unaware to My breath of Life as I breathe in your face and tell you, 'I love you, be still, don't be afraid.' Oh, how I long for you to once more know that I am here. Don't look from Me to find Me. I have not gone. I have not left you. Hear My voice, feel My breath, feel My arms around you. Don't strive to move from this place. This is the place where I can give you direction...Listen to My whispers in your ear as I hold you tight. Feel My arms around you. Feel My arms as I cradle, protect you, comfort you. From the first day I caught you I have not let you go. Relax...Wait, wait...Rest...rest...rest."

Wow! Is God amazing or what? I learned something important about listening in the night to hear what he has to say. That confirmation the next day was exactly what I needed to assure me that I was hearing Him and that it would be ok.

My beloved is unto me as a cluster of camphire in the vineyards of Engedi. (1:14)
Henna (camphire) in the Hebrew means the 'ransom price'. Henna flowers have great fragrance and beauty and the Jewish maidens would adorn themselves with them. En Gedi was a place in the wilderness of Judah where David fled to hide.

God is truly amazing, as we embrace myrrh with is preserving and healing qualities close to our hearts, outwardly He adorns us with His fragrant ransomed price for all to see.

We cannot adorn ourselves with a ransom paid, it is a supernatural adornment given by God for all to see. People in the world judge God by what they see in us. It only makes sense that he would adorn us in something so supernatural.

My husband always says that you can argue the scriptures but you cannot argue a changed man. As I began to die to myself and take the adornment of the Lord, I became changed for all to see. This adorning is done little by little, blossom by blossom. The Lord will not allow this sweetness to cover the vile smelling pieces of my life that gave into my own thoughts and ways. I needed to die to my old patterns for this adornment to come forth in that area. It is all a process that I believe will continue until I meet Jesus in the sky face to face.

During my journeys through dark times and wilderness, I have this precious bundle of myrrh in my heart. When I discern the sweetness of His presence and perfume, even in those times when I think I am alone, I suddenly become refreshed knowing He has paid a 'ransom price' for me. This was so supernatural; those who knew me could see that this could only be God.

Behold, thou art fair, my love; behold, thou art fair; thou hast doves' eyes. (1:15)
The original word fair means bright and beautiful. It was as if the Lord was looking upon me and saw in my heart that little bundle of myrrh and His atonement. He saw His own beauty and detected His fragrance. He said to me "Behold, you are fair, my love!"

But we all, with unveiled face, beholding as in a mirror the glory of the Lord, are being transformed into the same image from glory to glory, just as by the Spirit of the Lord. 2 Corinthians 3:18

I am so happy that the Lord does not look at my faults but sees the good in me. He sees all of us, as we will be. He says you 'have' dove's eyes. A dove not only represents the Holy Spirit but also is also very unique in the physical. A dove is faithful to one mate for life; they are totally devoted to each other. A dove (also called a Love Bird) has a binocular visual field, but is able to only put attention on one thing at a time. We are to have a single focus on our Lord. We are not to be like the daughters of Zion who walked with an outstretched neck and wanton eyes.

Moreover the LORD says: "Because the daughters of Zion are haughty, And walk with outstretched necks And wanton eyes, Walking and mincing [as] they go, Making a jingling with their feet. Isaiah 3:16

They were more focused on their outward appearance. We should not be looking at the world, desiring the flesh and man to meet our needs. When you have a lot of hurt in your life, it is sometimes hard not to reach for the quick fix the world offers. The world's fixes do not last, only allowing God to fix you will last. I can tell you that I had to lay down what others thought of me during this process.

A dove knows the seasons as the bride of Christ must know the seasons. This was my season for a deeper healing. We must have singleness of purpose in our vision, not allowing the world to take our focus away for our King. We must we have wide opened focused eyes, ready and waiting for the return of the bridegroom.

Behold, thou art fair, my beloved, yea, pleasant: also our bed is green. (1:16)

"It's not me who is fair. Remember I am dark. I know how shameful I feel when others look at the real me. I know how the sin of this world has scorched my heart. It is you, my love, who is the one of beauty. Without you, I am dark but with you I am lovely only because your beauty is upon me. You are so pleasing to my spirit, so agreeable to my heart. You are delightful not only to my eyes but to everything I am," I thought in my heart.

 Do you ever feel like that? So unworthy of how he sees you because you can only see the sin in your heart. Why do we have such a hard time accepting our true identity? I seem so undone when I am apart from Him, but when in Him I feel as if I can conquer anything!

As for me, I will see Your face in righteousness; I shall be satisfied when I awake in Your likeness. Psalm 17:15

This scripture has always been one of my favorites because so often I am so unsatisfied with my walk with God. I continually feel so unworthy but the truth is that I don't always believe what God sees in me.

Until the day I go to be with the Lord, I will continue to let go of my own thoughts towards myself and see what He sees. This is attainable for all of us……..to awake in His likeness! I have to learn that if I look in the physical, I see me. If I look in the Spirit, I see the truth…..His beauty is a true reflection upon me and through me.

I have a good friend who has helped me through so many of my hard times and helped me to see the truth of God in my life. One day as he prayed with me through a particularly hard time, he held my hand and wept as he prayed.

As my friend's tears hit my hand, I looked and I began to see my friend disappear and the image of Jesus became his image. The only part that I could see remaining of my friend was his shoes; the largest part of his image was the image of Jesus before me. Oh how I long to have His image upon me be so clear to others. This is the image of God's love as He meant us to see it working through everyday people just like us.

Although he does not point out that my fairness is just a reflection of him, I knew any beauty he sees is just a reflection. I am beginning to see the wonder of this the peace, the rest it brings to my soul. The bride declares "Yes, pleasant!" Pleasant are things that are pleasing to you. These things delight your heart and bring rest to you soul.

"Come to Me, all you who labor and are heavy laden, and I will give you rest." Matt 11:28

And He said, "My Presence will go with you, and I will give you rest." Exd 33:14

My heart is to get to the point when all the troubles of this world, which seem to keep coming, will not bring me down simply because I delight in Him.

Yea, though I walk through the valley of the shadow of death, I will fear no evil; For You are with me; Your rod and Your staff, they comfort me. Psalm 23:4

I will believe what He says and declare His goodness daily. One thing I did was to read the same scriptures over and over until they would become a reality in my heart.

Surely goodness and mercy shall follow me All the days of my life; And I will dwell in the house of the LORD Forever. Psalm 23:6

Our bed is green. Green is to be or grow exceedingly fertile or fresh or green. I am learning to grow in His rest, in the place He provides just for us together.

He makes me to lie down in green pastures; He leads me beside the still waters. Psalm 23:2

I am seeing that he would not lead me to a dry place to give me rest. In the heat of the day, in the heat of the troubles, he has a place of rest, just for me that will be refreshing and relaxing.

The beams of our house are cedar, and our rafters of fir. (1:17)
Why would it be cedar? The beams support the house.
Cedar is a lightweight and dimensionally stable wood that lies flat and stays straight, which means it resists the natural tendency to crack as you might find in many other wood species. Its distinct cell structure discourages rot from moisture by allowing it to dry out faster. Cedar fibers contain oils that act as natural preservatives to help the wood resist rot and decay and give off that distinct cedar aroma that is pleasant to humans but a deterrent to insects, moths and other wood pests. A cedar grows tall with deep roots to withstand the winds.

In the mountain of the height of Israel will I plant it: and it shall bring forth boughs, and bear fruit, and be a goodly cedar: and under it shall dwell all fowl of every wing; in the shadow of the branches thereof shall they dwell. Eze 17:23

This is the promise of God, I will plant in the highest place a cedar. To me this represents the man Jesus. What a foundation to hold up the structure of the house. No worm will work its way in and destroy the house.

The rafters are of fir, which is the best and strongest wood for roofing. The rafters bring stability to the structure. This was the best material to be used. If I am correct, the fir available to them was red fir. The red color of the fir represented the redemption of the cross. What a cool and pleasant place to find rest.

Chapter 3
Beginning to Understand

I am the rose of Sharon, and the lily of the valleys. (2:1)
There are a lot of different opinions on if this is the bride or bridegroom speaking here. In my heart I believe this is the Shulamite speaking. Sharon is a plain in Judea; the rose is a rambling rose or some ordinary flower that is common to the area. The Plain of Sharon was on the seacoast and many Gentiles lived there. A Gentile was anyone who was not a Jew. Sharon and the valleys are fertile places. She is saying that there is nothing special about her beauty; she is just an ordinary person in a good place. As a young Christian, I could not see anything special about me.

The growth of the lily, as that of all bulbous roots, is very quick and speedy. The root of the lily is in the ground all winter, but, when the moisture of the spring and with the warming of the soil, it starts growing quickly; so the grace of God changes the lives of those new in Him, sometimes very fast. The lily, when it has come to its full height is a lovely and faces downwards. The lily indeed grows fast, and grows fine, but it soon does not last long.

I love lilies and have them growing in my yard. My husband is not fond of them for the simple fact that they do not last. They enchant me. Nothing draws my senses as the lilies when they are in bloom. It seemed in my life I was growing so quickly that I would be like the lilies that I love and fade quickly. Therefore I seemed to hang my head, afraid to share much because it seems if I gave out, there would be nothing left. I did not realize that it is God who cares for the lilies of the field. I had so much to learn and understand.

As the lily among thorns, so is my love among the daughters. (2:2)
God was so gracious to me. In response to my thoughts on myself, he ignored what I had to say and brought light to my heart. It was as if He were saying to me, "Don't you see the lily hangs its head not in shame but because the true beauty is inward. Don't you see that you now stand tall in holiness and purity in the middle of a perverted and crooked generation?"

Consider the lilies how they grow: they toil not, they spin not; and yet I say unto you, that Solomon in all his glory was not arrayed like one of these. Luke 12:27

The lily is beautiful, it is tall and has six white pedals, and within those are seven grains of gold containing the pollen.
God is so purposeful in his designs. Six is the number of man and seven represents completion and spiritual perfection when referring to man.   He was saying me, "In the midst of where you grow, among the thorns of the earth, you stand high above in purity and grace. You will not be choked out. This is where my love lies." Why does he have to tell me things more than once? Will I ever get to the place where I just believe what he says?

As the apple tree among the trees of the wood, so is my beloved among the sons. I sat down under his shadow with great delight, and his fruit was sweet to my taste. (2:3)
All I can do is praise Him because still loves me with all my doubts. Can you imagine being in the woods, among all the tall and beautiful trees? You are in awe of all of them but you stumble upon one more precious than the rest, the one that will feed you.

To me it was like I had been searching through the forest of life, looking for the one that would bear sweet, nourishing, lasting fruit. I knew this fruit would prepare me for Eternity. My Jesus died so this tree would be planted here on earth for me to eat from anytime I want. I sat down and rested in His shade.

Keep me as the apple of Your eye; Hide me under the shadow of Your wings, From the wicked who oppress me, From my deadly enemies who surround me. Psalm 17:8-9

I had finally found my safe place in this world! I knew it was only here that I would not only find protection but victory from the enemy. I had found food, shelter and everything I needed. Never had I, in all my striving, ever found such a place. The longer I stayed under the shade of this Apple tree and began to trust in His protection, the greater my confidence and delight became.

Having come from the background of abuse it was very difficult to still myself many times in His presence. I had the fear that I was not safe. I would come up to the front of the church during worship seeking this shade and others who were excited about what God was doing, would begin to swarm around me. I understood that they just wanted to be where God was moving and at that moment was on me. But the having all people close to me frightened me badly. I was determined because of what I had found in His presence to find a way past this.

I talked with my Pastor, who was so gracious and understanding. He asked others in the church to give me some space. I had never had much trust in other people. I needed time to learn to trust my brothers and sisters. I needed time to trust that God would always be there when I came forward, that he would not abandon or hurt me.

One day as I was resting in this shade, God said to me, "You once were a victim. Then you became a survivor, now it the time for you to become an overcomer!"

"He who overcomes shall inherit all things, and I will be his God and he shall be My son." Rev. 21:7

From that day on my life changed. I realized that I didn't need a miracle.....I needed to become the miracle! All for the glory to One who saved me and protected me. You can't go back and start over but you can make a new ending---starting from where you are right now. His fruit had become the sweetest I had ever tasted. I would let him change anything in me, if He would only allow me to continue to come and sit in the shade and taste of the fruit. Many people in the church call this "soaking" in His presence. It is a stilling of your mind and heart and listening, waiting for Him to come. This is one of my favorite places to be but yet I knew there was more to know about my bridegroom.

He brought me to the banqueting house, and his banner over me was love. (2:4)
I think may Christians do not truly understand what it means to be brought into the banqueting house. It was a journey to get to the point that the Lord could bring me in.

In the beginning I had some incredible experiences with him. I longed for a closer walk with Him. I had some very sweet encounters with my Lord and He brought me into the chambers. He put a hunger and a thirst deep within my soul, so much that I cried out for Him to "Kiss me" and "draw me". I ran after Him and he brought me to His table. I learned to feed off him and to rest in His presence. But the former table is not the same as this one.

Banqueting house literally means house of wine. Wine symbolizes joy. This house, this place is very special; it is a place that only the Lord can bring you into when you are able to understand. This is a place of incredible joy because here I was given a greater revelation of His love. I know I only understand a small portion of the height and depth of his love.

"That He would grant you, according to the riches of His glory, to be strengthened with might through His Spirit in the inner man, that Christ may dwell in your hearts through faith; that you, being rooted and grounded in love, may be able to comprehend with all the saints what is the width and length and depth and height—to know the love of Christ which passes knowledge; that you may be filled with all the fullness of God." Eph 3:16-19

Unfortunately too many turn down the invitation to the banqueting house. They seem satisfied to feed off the tree, never understanding the fullness of why the tree is there. The banqueting house is for those who are following hard after His love, those that have lost sight of all the other things; those who are willing to go all the way no matter what the price. "Are you willing to go into the banqueting house?"

"For which of you, intending to build a tower, does not sit down first and count the cost, whether he has enough to finish it" Luke 14:28

Sometimes when we ask God for things and we don't count the cost of what we are asking for. We all want to have a great anointing, to reflect Jesus in our lives, to do the works, to bring the lost to the Lord. We can pray great prayers...they sound so good....but are we willing to pay the price.

I see so many people who pray but have no action. (Please note: I do not in any way mean to devalue prayer, it is of greatest importance.) But I believe many of us are called to put action to our prayers. We are to pray but we are to press and walk into our callings. I am tired of hearing cries of prayer such as...."Save our city, Lord" or "God give me your fullness", with no intension of moving with God. We are God's hands on this earth. He works through us. We are called to intercede but we are also called to go higher and out into the fields. There is a cost.

"But I say to you that for every idle word men may speak, they will give account of it in the Day of Judgment." Matthew 12:36

Idle means empty, unused, averse to labor, vain. Do you think we could pray idle prayers? I am not even close to be perfect in my walk but I think I have always been very aware of the price of what I ask for. Salvation is free, but there is a price to go higher. The Lord spoke to me the other night about the price. This is what I heard.

"There is no mercy or no grace in the price. The price is simply what it is. The price is everything....everything you have been, everything you are and everything you will be. There are no shortcuts, no discounts for works, the price is what it is......EVERYTHING. I will give you mercy and grace as you come to give yourself to me, but the price will always be...everything. Give me everything of you and I in return will give you the FULLNESS OF ME."

It doesn't matter who you are or where you live, if you choose to pay the price, His banner of love waves over you. We do not always see it, but believe me it is there.

Not only does this banner of love show that we belong to him, but the protection that His love brings is also ours. In a battle there is great importance in capturing the enemy's flag or banner. Satan would like nothing more than to have that banner of His love removed from our lives. You need to go to the banqueting house and obtain the banner of love! If you choose to give yourself up to Him completely, He will bring you into the banqueting house and great joy will be yours.

Stay me with flagons, comfort me with apples: for I am sick of love. (2:5)

This revelation of His love was too overwhelming for me to fully understand. The hunger and yearning in my heart seemed to increase which I in no way could have imagined would have been possible. I cried out to Him, "Do not take away this revelation of your love, but I am afraid it is too much to endure unless you give me strength." It seems that a cry had come out me that expressed a love I had never experienced before. I was lovesick.

The Spirit of His love was so heavy on me; it actually was pleasantly exhausting to my physical body. I could not seem to react normal to anything around me. I would come home from church on Sunday morning and be in a daze until I could return again that evening. I understand why God just does not just bring us all immediately into the banqueting house. It would be too much to bear. There must be a preparation in your heart to be able to endure being sick with love.

I just seemed to want more. He became my obsession. I found myself crying out, "Feed me more!" Although I went to work, cleaned my house and did the general things you must do each day, he was constantly on my mind. In my mind, I tried to figure out how to get more of Him.

How I could manage to sneak in a little closer? I still had so much more to learn about love. An incredible experience is only a compliment to a lifetime of learning to recognize the love of God that is in our lives each and every day.

His left hand is under my head, and his right hand doth embrace me. (2:6)
I am beginning to see how he holds me up. Many people say that the left hand represents the anger and wrath of God. I tend to think of it more as discipline with love. I would call it tough love. The left hand can be gentle if you are willing to receive it. My love for Him now gives me a fear that is healthy but yet I still need Him to shape my life. As a child I never received much discipline and although it is sometimes hard to take, I know it is for my good. If the left hand is under your head, it puts a picture in my mind of a reclining position where the head (your mind) is not being held up by the neck (your will).

The right hand symbolizes the pure love of God and grace and it embraces me. The left hand disciplines my mind yet the right hand embraces me with love and grace. I don't know about you but this is the way I believe our bridegroom wishes to change our lives.

I charge you, O ye daughters of Jerusalem, by the roes, and by the hinds of the field, that ye stir not up, nor awake my love, till he please. (2:7)
It was if the Lord was saying to me, "Be careful to walk softly and wait on me. Charging in and trying to hurry things will be like coming upon a deer quickly; it will flee. I know what is best for you and it is I who chooses when I will share with you. I set this time as a time of rest to regain your strength."

I have found that too many times our friends meaning well, will try to rush us along as if we need to catch up with them. We all run a race at our own pace and no one's path is the same. We need to listen to the Holy Spirit and let him be our guide.

I had to remember that just one movement of my flesh could disturb this incredible intimate place in which he had me at this moment. It was not that he would not ever bring me here again but this moment, this place was very pleasing to Him and His joy is my strength.

Return to your rest, O my soul, For the LORD has dealt bountifully with you. Psalm 116:7

There were lots of people in the church that had suggestions on how I could overcome my pain and not have to spend so much time on the floor in the presence of God. They did not understand that what they saw as a great weakness was a great empowering in my life.

The one thing I know is you have to listen to God first and follow His steps, rest when he tells you to rest and run when he tells you to run. Doing this will definitely help you overcome the fear of man. Now there is wise counsel to listen to but just because a person is in the church does not necessarily mean that they have wise counsel for your situation. Wise Godly counsel comes from the heart of God through the vessel he chooses.

You will show me the path of life; In Your presence is fullness of joy; At Your right hand are pleasures forevermore. Psalm 16:11

The voice of my beloved! behold, he cometh leaping upon the mountains, skipping upon the hills. (2:8)

There will be a time during that time of rest when all of the sudden, you hear His voice. I could suddenly see a clearer picture of this resurrection life he had given me. I could see Him leaping upon the mountains of my life, skipping upon those low valleys with no effort. In my heart it was as if He was calling me to come out and see that He would teach me His ways. He would mold me into His image so I could become surefooted in Him. There are so many seasons in our lives. As a dove knows the seasons, do we recognize the seasons in our lives? Even after all I had experienced, I still found that it was not always easy following that voice.

To everything there is a season, A time for every purpose under heaven Ecc 3:1

My beloved is like a roe or a young hart: behold, he standeth behind our wall, he looketh forth at the windows, shewing himself through the lattice. (2:9)
It seemed that nothing could stop His drawing of me, even my lack of complete trust in Him. The problem was that somehow there seemed to be a wall between us. Notice this scripture does not say "my" wall but "our" wall meaning that wall belonged to both the bride and the bridegroom, at least this is the way the bride sees it. I didn't see the wall as a problem at all.

I intended for this wall to enclose my Lord and me together and to keep the world out. I never wanted to have the world be a part of my life; I had spent my entire life putting distance between the world and I. All I wanted at this point was to have this wonderful intimate fellowship with the Lord, rest in Him and live happily ever after in these walls. I had found the Lord in my heart all the time and I still wanted to ignore circumstances, people, and the many trials of life.

I could not see that by always turning inward to seek the joy of His presence that I was depriving the world of what the Lord was putting inside me. That was my wall.

I couldn't see ever having anything of value to say that anyone would want to listen to. Also I still hadn't quite gotten past the old mindset that if you attracted attention to yourself, it would end in hurt and possibly physical pain. It had always been a wise choice to remain invisible to the world.

Then while I was on the floor in His presence he spoke a truth into my life. He sent me to Luke 8:47, he said "You are like that certain woman for the power has gone out of me and is healing you; you can no longer remain hidden."

Now when the woman saw that she was not hidden, she came trembling; and falling down before Him, she declared to Him in the presence of all the people the reason she had touched Him and how she was healed immediately. Luke 8:47

I did not yet have the revelation of the body of Christ and how we each have something of value. I was like that woman, I wanted to take the healing, the touch and run and hide to enjoy the healing myself. She had suffered so much rejection; I believe she may have had the same mindset as me. Then He sent me to the two greatest commandments.

"And the second, like it, is this: 'You shall love your neighbor as yourself.' There is no other commandment greater than these." Mark 12:31

I thought, "How could I love my neighbor enough to share if I do not even love myself?" But how do you learn to love yourself? It is a really hard thing, even scary, to accept who you are completely.
I think many times we are our own worst enemy. I think that making a decision to love myself was a decision to want to come to a fuller life than I have ever experienced. I had to realize I was unique and not a mistake. God does not make mistakes! I would speak to myself the truths He had spoken to me, "He created me for a purpose and I am perfect for that. I have great value in the kingdom and nothing can change that! I was created in His image."

We are not talking about pride here but learning a genuine happiness and acceptance in the beauty that God has created in me. There are many areas in my life that did not even come into the picture here. Who I was on the inside was important, not what I did for a living or how I looked or where I lived. I had to see God has put something so special inside of me, just not only for me but for the world because He loves the world and me. God cares so much for me that he has numbered the hairs on my head. He loves me; shouldn't I learn to love myself? I wanted to love the things of this world that He loves and that included me.

Somehow I needed to find a way to let go of my intense need to keep His love all to myself and allow him to lead me out into the view of anyone he wanted. He was not resting behind the wall but standing and He was on the outside. In standing he was showing me that He would not rest while there was still a work to be done in my life. I realized I could not keep Him inside the wall.

He had stayed inside this wall with me as I learned to love Him but now it was time to trust Him outside my wall.

I needed to learn to live by something else than just the feeling of His presence, more than just knowing His presence in a certain time and place while I was seeking Him.

Did you notice the windows and the lattice? God always finds a way to enlighten the heart of the ones who have set themselves apart for Him. The Lord was trying to deliver me from my wall. He wanted me to learn that His presence could be found in any circumstance; there was no longer a need to just look within myself. My God is bigger than that. He is omnipresent. As long as I looked inward and only concentrated on my own personal feeling of joy, I would never understand His calling to come out.

My beloved spake, and said unto me, Rise up, my love, my fair one, and come away. (2:10)

It couldn't have been clearer to me; he really was calling me out of my wonderful secure place. I thought, "Doesn't He know that this is the only real security I have ever felt? And He is asking me to leave?" There was the season facing me again. I was facing a new growing time in my life. Somehow I knew if I remained where I was I would miss His fullness that I was seeking.

I had found a peace that I had never known before. I could finally sleep at night without waking up and walking around the house, making sure no one was there and the doors were secure. I was so afraid if I stepped out that I would lose the peace and joy I had found. Still I could not quite wrap my mind around the covering that His love provided me.

It wasn't that all those inward experiences were wrong, they are still precious to me, but I could not continue in that way. Then He spoke to me, "Don't you see that I am looking for a relationship that surpasses just feelings? I want to relate to you in the Spirit." What could that mean? Wasn't being in His presence like being in the Spirit? There was a whole new realm that I was about to learn about.

For, lo, the winter is past, the rain is over and gone; (2:11)
He was calling me to leave my past experiences, both the bad and the good. I was not to forget the past but I could not continue live in it. At this point my past still dominated my life. I needed to die to my old life and become new in Him. I needed to strive for higher and new experiences in Him. I needed to change.

Just as the leaves surrender their leaves to the seasons,
So I desire for you to surrender those things in your life
Which need to be surrendered to the season.
You think the trees are left bare,
But there is a work ..
A preparation that is taking place deep within the roots,
Getting ready for new growth.
I see such beauty in change.
As you walk out the door and see the leaves,
See the beauty in change,
The beauty in surrendering.

The flowers appear on the earth; the time of the singing of birds is come, and the voice of the turtle is heard in our land; The fig tree putteth forth her green figs, and the vines with the tender grape give a good smell. Arise, my love, my fair one, and come away. (2:12-13)

When the flowers begin to show their faces it is a true sign that the winter is over. The rains of spring prepare the ground for the flowers to shoot sprouts. He began showing me all the growth in this new resurrection life that was before me. I was beginning to turn my sight from that dead past life and starting to look forward.

It was still a struggle to keep that sight when hard things came before me. To learn about singing, I began to hear the Lord singing to me while I worshiped.
I sing over Him and then in return He sings over me. To some this may seem hard to imagine but Jesus is our model, right?

Jesus says in John 5:19 "I tell you the truth, the Son can do nothing by himself; he can do only what he see his Father doing, because whatever the Father does the Son does. For the Father loves the Son and shows him all he does." Since the word is telling us to worship God, to sing to Him songs. I knew that He must have been singing also.

Zephaniah 3:17 "The Lord your God is with you, he is mighty to save. He will take great delight in you, he will quiet you with his love, he will rejoice over you with singing."

Interesting that to "rejoice over you with singing" or "rinnah" (rin-naw) is a ringing cry, a cry of passion. Like in Psalm 126:5 "Those who sow in tears will reap with songs of joy" or Isaiah when talking of the joy of the redeemed in 35:10.."They will enter Zion with singing; everlasting joy will crown their heads."

There is no way to describe the passion I heard. You need to hear Him sing for yourself. No one sings like the Lord. We were singing a song called 'Here I am to worship', which has a line that says, "I'll never know how much it cost, to see my sin upon that cross." As I sang I pondered on the reality of that line. Then I heard the Lord speak to me. He said, "You will never know how much it cost but that cost is my wedding gift to you." Then He began to sing....
So here I am to love you, Here I am to hold you,
Here I am to say that you're My bride. You're altogether lovely, Altogether worthy, Altogether wonderful to Me. You'll never know how much it cost to see your sin upon My cross. So here I am to love you.......

The next evening I came to church feeling hurt and a bit beat up by something someone had done to me. Then the Lord began to sing sweetly into my heart again. This time He changed just one word but it changed my whole attitude. He sang...You'll never know how much it cost to feel your sin upon My cross. So here I am to love you, Here I am to hold you, Here I am to say that you're My bride. My hurt feelings just faded away. God's love is greater than we could ever imagine!

Isaiah 62 :5b..."as a bridegroom rejoices over his bride, so will your God rejoice over you."

The turtledove is a symbol of love and of the Holy Spirit. The turtledove is one of the first birds to return in the spring, returning to the warmth of the returning sun. I was beginning to feel the genuine warmth of His love and began to freely return it. It was like springtime in my life. Things began to grow and bud. Not yet producing fruit but heading in the right direction.

"Now learn this parable from the fig tree: When its branch has already become tender and puts forth leaves, you know that summer is near. So you also, when you see all these things, know that it is near — at the doors!" Matt 24:32-33

When will we hear that shout? When will he come to gather us up? We cannot stay in the winter of our lives; we must be ready. The vine, the true vine, with its tender fruit gives a sweet smell. What good is a blossom in the spring if it bears no fruit? It may be beautiful but the goal is to produce fruit. Again he is calling, rise up and come away. This is almost too much to bear. All the changes in my life seem to be happening so rapidly. I still wonder how I will ever bear fruit worthy for the King?

O my dove, that art in the clefts of the rock, in the secret places of the stairs, let me see thy countenance, let me hear thy voice; for sweet is thy voice, and thy countenance is comely. (2:14)
He was calling me, reminding me, of a position that I was about to obtain in spite of my doubts. He called me a dove, which said to me that I would be manifesting the full life of the Spirit. How could I manifest what I did not really understand? Before He had only told me I had dove's eyes, where did I change? He was seeing me with eyes of faith. Oh how I wish to see others around me with those eyes.

What could the cleft of the rock be? Is it a cave? I thought he didn't want me to hide anymore. Then He gave me a vision of the cross and suddenly I understood. Jesus is the Rock of my salvation and the clefts is his beautiful side pierced just for me. It was almost unbearable to handle just one glimpse of pure love. I could see that secret place where I could hide is difference from places I use to hide because the place I could now hide is in Him.

"So it shall be, while My glory passes by, that I will put you in the cleft of the rock, and will cover you with My hand while I pass by." Exd 33:22

In the Spirit I am safe in the cleft of the rock. God protects me from things that would otherwise consume me. Only through Christ can I have the knowledge of the glory of God. No one can see His glory in their comfort zone but those who rise and stand upon this rock, and take shelter in it will see.

He is calling me to look up so He can see my face. I need to keep my face turned towards heaven and not towards this world. He said to me, "If you look up, you will never walk in darkness again, for I am the light."
I still was having a hard time fully believing that my voice would be sweet to Him. How could He see me as lovely? I was still looking at my flesh and not the Spirit. I had so much more to learn.

Take us the foxes, the little foxes, that spoil the vines: for our vines have tender grapes. (2:15)
He was calling me to get up and take care of the vineyard of my soul. It wasn't enough to sit and admire the beauty around me, to smell the blossoms. I love to rest and listen to the birds sing but it was time for me to be a partaker in the keeping of the vineyard of my soul.

If you have ever been around foxes, you know they always take away the fruit. They only want the fruit and do not care if they break the branches or if there will ever be a chance of the vine bearing fruit again. If foxes are unnoticed they will destroy the fruit. If unwatched or unguarded little things can ruin it all. In a vineyard the caretaker is vital in catching the foxes.

What are the little foxes? They are small manifestations, habits and thoughts of my old life. He was telling me if I was not careful, the vines could be destroyed. I was instructed to listen and do what the caretaker told me to do. The caretaker of my soul is the Holy Spirit. The word spoil means strangle. It's the things I consider 'little sins' and neglect that strangle the vine in my life, cutting off that flow of life from the branch which is Jesus Christ.

My beloved is mine, and I am his: he feedeth among the lilies. (2:16)
Wow, He is mine! I was finally beginning to see what I thought was the truth. This is a truth but seen in a very selfish light. See at this point, it is still I that is first in my life. It's what I get first and what he gets second.
There still much more of the dance to be danced before I can change this mindset of mine. I need to realize the importance that I was created for him.

I did understand that He could be found among the lilies, his people, feeding his flock. I am not offended anymore to be a part of this flock and follow their lead in things I do not understand. The Holy Spirit was beginning to confirm in my heart that the direction I was heading was correct, but I had not arrived yet.

Until the day break, and the shadows flee away, turn, my beloved, and be thou like a roe or a young hart upon the mountains of Bether. (2:17)

I found myself putting my conditions for my comfort zone upon Him. I was saying, "Someday, I'll be His delight and skip with him on the mountains, but not now. Life is too hard. I need to protect myself and hide behind my wall."

How many times has He called me out already, once……..twice? I was still living in fear, wanting to wait until everything is out in the light and there are no shadows or darkness to scare me. Have you ever done that?

I cried out to Him just like a freighted child, "I know Lord you have already healed so much in my life but can you just give me a little more time. Please come back when I can see things clearly in the light. I see you jumping from mountain top to mountain top, I am afraid I will stumble in the dim light."   I had always thought; how could the children of Israel see so much of God's power and still not trust Him? Here I was in the same position.

"God please help me overcome my lack of trust in you. Help me to quit putting my needs and delights first.
I truly do want to believe and rely upon you only, but somehow my flesh keeps getting in the way. I know that there will be many challenges in my life with this prayer. After all I am asking for you to change me. Please give me the strength to face these challenges. But most of all, please never stop drawing or calling me out, even if I do not come at first. I do love you but I know my loves needs to grow. Don't give up on me Lord, I'm coming!"

Chapter 4
Did He Leave Me?

By night on my bed I sought him whom my soul loveth: I sought him, but I found him not. (3:1)

In this instance the Lord is birthing a hunger in his Bride to seek him. She has been waiting in the darkness for the first rays of dawn. In the previous chapter she puts a condition on her comfort zone. He has called her out. (2:10) "Arise my darling, my beautiful one and come with me". He calls her out twice. In verse 2:16 she proclaims, "My lover is mine and I am his." But she adds in the next verse "until the day breaks and the shadows flee." She chose to stay in the safety of her darkness. So in order to draw her out, he has to create a greater hunger in her heart. In order to create that greater hunger, He withdraws the feeling of his presence from her. This creates that greater hunger that draws her into the light.

I identified with the bride here. One day there came a point in my life where I could not seem to find God in the familiar patterns I had used before. I would come into the church and trying as hard as I could, it just did not feel the same. "Did he leave me?" I knew this was not true but that is what it felt like. I was blind to the fact that He was calling me into a new season, a new time of maturing. I could not see that I was only seeking Him in the time of rest. He wanted me to see that everything did not have to be completely right in my life to step out with Him.

When I remember You on my bed, I meditate on You in the night watches. Psalm 63:6

Somehow I could focus more on Him in the night watch than in the normal hours of the days; before he had been constantly on my mind. It seemed something had changed.

"Was I losing my passion or did His presence make Him so much more real to me before? Why would His presence leave me?" This was all so confusing to me. I wanted to live in the place I had been before with Him, that was enough to satisfy me. I just could not see the entire picture. Remaining in that particular spot really was just surviving. He wanted me to overcome!

I had a few choices at this point either go out and find Him, become bitter because He left or just give up and go back to my former life. Don't think that just going out and getting high didn't sound tempting, but the reality to that was I might as well jump off a cliff and end my life. Going back to the past would mean certain death. Light is a scary place if you have never lived in it. All I could think was, "How could you love me? I have so little faith and trust in You." The time had come to make the decision on which way I would go. I think so many people choose to stop at this point. There is a sick sort of comfort in your pain. Pain is not a place we are not meant to stay in.

I will rise now, and go about the city in the streets, and in the broad ways I will seek him whom my soul loveth: I sought him, but I found him not. (3:2)
The choice is made; I will go out and find Him. Finding someone that I really didn't understand yet is not as easy as I thought. The only thing I knew was to look in the places common to my knowledge. Sometimes you have to go beyond the common places in your life to find the one you love. I began to retrace the footsteps in my life.

"Where was the place I first met Him? Perhaps that is place I need to be." I headed for the sanctuary. Something was missing and I could not understand why He was not in the place I had always found Him.

This growing love inside me was pushing me on in desperation. Life was not worth living if I could not find Him.

I could not see that He never left; I was only looking in my comfortable places. He could be found if I would choose to step out of my comfort zone and into places I had never desired to go to before. It was humbling to know that the thing in my life that I did not want to deal with was the pathway where He was waiting for me. I needed to change my mindset on where I would find Him.

The watchmen that go about the city found me: to whom I said, Saw ye him whom my soul loveth? (3:3)
A good watchman in the church sees something is not right and will go check it out and send what help is needed. These precious saints knew something was going on and tried to help. I was desperate; had they seen Him? I had such respect for these saints but why couldn't they help? I loved these people and all the help they had given me but what they had to give at that moment was not enough. I had realized that there was a meeting place, a pathway where nobody could walk along with me and no one else could understand. It was my path that only I could choose to go down it.

It was but a little that I passed from them, but I found him whom my soul loveth: I held him, and would not let him go, until I had brought him into my mother's house, and into the chamber of her that conceived me. (3:4)

It was my decision to go down that dreaded path alone. It was so scary but as I began to walk, it was not long before I found Him again. The One I had thought I had lost was there with His arms open wide.

I have always said that my favorite scripture is found in the Song of Songs 3:4 … When I found the one I love.
I held him and would not let him go. I speak it constantly and everyone who knows me has heard it, if not more than once. The Holy Spirit said to me one day..."You forgot the rest of the scripture. It's time to move into a deeper relationship." Of course I thought, "What? There's more to it?" Ever done that? The rest reads... Until I had brought him to the house of my mother, And into the chamber of her who conceived me.

Suddenly I realized that the reason I was holding so tightly to the Lord was because I was afraid if I let go, he would leave me. I needed to learn to trust his love. This love is a hard area for me but I am learning. I cannot tell you how many times I had been abandoned in my life. I realized those fears existed in my relationship with God. Doesn't this sound like a clinging immature bride who does not realize the deep commitment her husband has for her?

I had been hearing a call for several months...Rise up and be who you are called to be! I am not called to be a clinging bride but a functional one. I was afraid to step too far out of my comfort zone for fear that somehow God would be displeased with something I did and leave. The key word that stands out to me is that little one "until". It says there's more to it. As love grows and you mature you don't have to physically cling to one another every minute. You are a team. There is a trust, something much deeper...you carry each other in your hearts. Your souls are united.

Take a look at a child. At first they cling to their mothers. As they grow, they realize that they can move out a little from her to discover and develop into who they are. They know she is watching over them.   Until....I brought him into my mother's house...my beginnings, my roots. We must bring the Lord into our homes and our hearts....but it goes deeper yet...and into the chamber of the one who conceived me....the place of intimacy. There is freedom in intimacy with God.

Who can separate us from the love of Christ?   Shall tribulation, or distress, or peril or sword? Romans 8:35

For you were like sheep going astray, but now have returned to the Shepard and Overseer of your souls. 1Peter 2:25

I pondered on this. According to Strong's an overseer here indicates the character of the work overtaken. God is like the mother who watches over her child, yet gives him the freedom to grow, to develop, to learn. He loves us so much that he puts up with us lovingly in our immaturity.

The kingdom of God really must not make sense to the wise men of this world. I am not saying here to let go of God but to hold onto him in our hearts. To stand, you must lie down; to seek, you must turn away. To stand in Christ you lay down the world. To seek him you must turn away from the things of this world and old mindsets. To come in, you must go out. To come into the kingdom, you must go out of the worldly ways. This is the path I am now choosing to walk. It is a walk out of the past into my future. He had not tested me beyond what I could bear.

I charge you, O ye daughters of Jerusalem, by the roes, and by the hinds of the field, that ye stir not up, nor awake my love, till he please. (3:5)

This is the same warning as before but now it takes on a different light. I had been before really only concerned about my joy and my communion with my Lord. I had said that this place was very pleasing to Him and His joy is my strength. The truth was that it was pleasing to me. Yes, He was pleased but my heart was still seeking my own needs first. Now I truly was beginning to see His needs first. He had such a need to spend time with me beyond my wall that He would take the time to draw me out.

His love is so strong that His desire was for me to choose the hard path that led to Him and He knew the perfect time for me to begin walking. Only with this deeper calling into unity with Him and walking together, could I walk down this path to my destiny. I was beginning to see that if I followed His lead; no steps would be missed and no toes would be stepped on.

Who is this that cometh out of the wilderness like pillars of smoke, perfumed with myrrh and frankincense, with all powders of the merchant? (3:6)
I had been walking through one of the hardest paths in my life. I felt as if I could not take another step but my love was pulling my heart forward. I was a desperate, desolate, and broken woman. I had been weeping before the saints, "Have you found the one I love?" I normally am not an overly emotional person. This whole episode of walking out of my comfort zone had turned my life and emotions upside down. I even wondered if I could survive this.

I had felt that if I could not find Him, my past would devour me. The pain I had felt was overwhelming. A life time of hurt seemed to be the path I had been walking through, reliving so much which I had put out of my mind for so many years.

When I saw Him standing there, arms open wide, I got a revelation of what love is, greater than I had ever known. I saw the pain of my past, which I had just walked through, was the preparation for my future. I had reconciled myself with my past in order to make my future more fruitful.

Together we would walk out of that wilderness in His glory, perfumed with the sweet smell of death to my flesh. I had the smell of the powder of the redeemed. I had been purchased with the price of His love.

This was not about me but the revelation of what He chose to give up so I could reach this point. This was not the end of dealing with my past but after this point, I cannot even explain why, but for some reason the deep unbearable pain left my heart.

You know my sitting down and my rising up; You understand my thought afar off. You comprehend my path and my lying down, and are acquainted with all my ways. Psalm 139:2-3

Behold his bed, which is Solomon's; threescore valiant men are about it, of the valiant of Israel. They all hold swords, being expert in war: every man hath his sword upon his thigh because of fear in the night. (3:7-8)

We were walking yet my spirit was at rest knowing that I was protected. Just like Solomon who would lie on his couch and rest as he traveled knowing that the sixty valiant men would protect him. I had no clue as to how much of a battle had been fought in the Spirit just to bring me to this point. The night had caused me so much fear in my life, yet suddenly I knew that my King was here for me to protect from the fear of the night. I would never fear as I had before. This protection was a side of love I had never seen before. I didn't quite know how to process in my mind that someone would actually fight and protect me. I never learned this growing up. What a load lifted off my shoulders knowing that I did not have to run in fear any longer. The battle was no longer mine.

He has redeemed my soul in peace from the battle that was against me, for there were many against me. Psalm 55:18

King Solomon made himself a chariot of the wood of Lebanon. He made the pillars thereof of silver, the bottom thereof of gold, the covering of it of purple, the midst thereof being paved with love, for the daughters of Jerusalem (3:9-10)
I could see it now. It was the bridegroom himself who designed the transportation to bring his bride home. It was made of the finest wood that had to be cut, shaped and formed for this purpose. The pillars were of silver, which is redemption and supports of gold or divine nature. The seat is of purple which represents Kingly authority. The interior paved with love, this was my covering.

All this had been designed just for me. Jesus was the cedar planted in the highest place above Israel. The tree was cut, redemption and His divine nature was my transportation. He sat me upon His kingly authority and covered me in love. This would all bring me directly to the wedding.

"When I passed by you again and looked upon you, indeed your time was the time of love; so I spread My wing over you and covered your nakedness. Yes, I swore an oath to you and entered into a covenant with you, and you became Mine," says the Lord GOD. Eze 16:8

Go forth, O ye daughters of Zion, and behold king Solomon with the crown wherewith his mother crowned him in the day of his espousals, and in the day of the gladness of his heart. (3:11)

I wanted everyone to see what I was seeing. Go all of you who are close to Him, down the path He chooses for you. Meet Him and get the revelation of His love.

My Jesus wore a crown of thorns placed there by the ones He loved, humanity. This was His wedding day. The wedding present given to us that was the greatest gift. This was not only His day of greatest pain but also the day of gladness in His heart.

I think too many of us are waiting for the wedding. We do not understand the betrothal that has taken place between Jesus and ourselves.

"Let us be glad and rejoice and give Him glory, for the marriage of the Lamb has come, and His wife has made herself ready." Rev 19:7

Betrothal was much more than what we see as an engagement today. Joseph considered the option of divorcing Mary. Today a divorce takes place after the marriage. The bride and groom had to remain faithful to each other for a year before the actual marriage ceremony took place. I could see clearly now that He already had taken me as His wife and soon He would come and get me with the transportation He built to bring me to the wedding ceremony. Until then as I travel through life I must remain faithful to Him and make myself ready.

Chapter 5
How God Sees Us

I was helping to teach a bible study on the Song of Songs and when I got to chapter 4, I thought, "There is so much symbolism here Lord. How do I convey this easily to the ladies without spending weeks teaching them all the symbolism?" Here is what he gave me. This how God sees you and me! You may not be there, but who is? God sees you as you will be! I thought God was just giving me a wonderful thing for the bible study. I did not find out until I stopped writing what this would mean to me and the chance I would have to grow.

Behold, thou art fair, my love; behold, thou art fair; thou hast doves' eyes within thy locks: thy hair is as a flock of goats, that appear from mount Gilead. (4:1)
How incredibly beautiful you are my most precious one. Your eyes have been opened to great spiritual insight and you focus only on me. You see the light of the gospel; the glory of God is in your sight. You are separated unto a life with your God and I am your strength. You come forward unto me as a living sacrifice, how beautiful that is, entire surrender.

Thy teeth are like a flock of sheep that are even shorn, which came up from the washing; whereof every one bear twins, and none is barren among them. (4:2)
You have matured and able to partake of the strong meat of the word. You have removed the toil (sweat) of this world with the washing of my word. Your mind is being renewed. You are being freed from the wisdom of this world and renewed in the wisdom and knowledge of God. There is a balance in the wisdom and knowledge of God in you. You hold onto former truths yet reaching out for and learning to walk in new truth and understanding. Your meat is to do the will of God in your life.

Thy lips are like a thread of scarlet, and thy speech is comely: thy temples are like a piece of a pomegranate within thy locks. (4:3)

Your lips bring redemption and deliverance to men. Your lips are lovely and do not speak proud and profane things but have been redeemed and delivered for my service. Your thoughts are opened and exposed to God, yet veiled from the outward world. You have allowed me to search your heart and your thoughts and my light has shone through them.

Thy neck is like the tower of David builded for an armoury, whereon there hang a thousand bucklers, all shields of mighty men. (4:4)

Your will is in submission to my will. Your strength is found in a heart that is submitted to follow my heart. Your armor is your faith in your God, which shall withstand all that is thrown at you. You have been trained in love and radiate kingly authority. The Spirit of God in the resurrection power leads you.

Thy two breasts are like two young roes that are twins, which feed among the lilies. (4:5)

You bear the inward qualities of faith and love, which have developed in balance. You can discern or judge between good and evil. Feeding in my pastures perfects faith and love.

Until the day break, and the shadows flee away, I will get me to the mountain of myrrh, and to the hill of frankincense. (4:6)

You have at last agreed to come with me to the place of death to your fleshly life until the light takes away all darkness and the fragrance is sweet. This is the intimacy I desire.

Thou art all fair, my love; there is no spot in thee. (4:7)

You are more beautiful than you can imagine. I see nothing wrong with you. You are a perfect sacrifice, beautiful in my eyes.

Come with me from Lebanon, my spouse, with me from Lebanon: look from the top of Amana, from the top of Shenir and Hermon, from the lions' dens, from the mountains of the leopards. (4:8)
I am pleased to call you my Bride, come with me to the highest, most beautiful places and see things the way I see them. Look with me from the high places, from the hiding of the enemy, from the places of battle and the places of sanctuary and together we will see the Promised Land. This is the place of intimacy I wish to share with my bride.

Thou hast ravished my heart, my sister, my spouse; thou hast ravished my heart with one of thine eyes, with one chain of thy neck. (4:9)
I am so pleased with your love that my heart beats faster. Through the glance of your eyes, I see your soul and my heart beats even faster with love for you. With one "yes", my heart beats fast with love.

How fair is thy love, my sister, my spouse! how much better is thy love than wine! and the smell of thine ointments than all spices! (4:10)
My bride you are so close to me, your love is my delight. Our love is greater than joy; it is the delight of my heart. The release of your spirit life brings forth a great and pleasant fragrance to me. The fragrance of the brokenness in your life is the sweetest smell of all.

Thy lips, O my spouse, drop as the honeycomb: honey and milk are under thy tongue; and the smell of thy garments is like the smell of Lebanon. (4:11)

I have found my promise land in you through great intimacy. The fragrance of your outward attitudes and behaviors, your everyday ministry and life in me puts off a fragrance to be compared to the most beautiful of places.

A garden inclosed is my sister, my spouse; a spring shut up, a fountain sealed. (4:12)

You have an inward place of beauty that is reserved only for my pleasure, set apart for me. This is a place we walk and fellowship intimately together. There is pure water there, not polluted but set apart only for me.

Thy plants are an orchard of pomegranates, with pleasant fruits; camphire, with spikenard, Spikenard and saffron; calamus and cinnamon, with all trees of frankincense; myrrh and aloes, with all the chief spices: (4:13-14)

This place, this garden is a paradise of Godly thoughts. The fruit of the Spirit in your life is bringing forth fruit unto your life. You are being transformed into my image from glory to glory. You are a holy meeting place for me alone. Your life filled with praise to God is a sweet fragrance. You have brought forth the quality of suffering love as you follow your Lover.

A fountain of gardens, a well of living waters, and streams from Lebanon. (4:15)

Because you have believed on me, rivers of living waters shall flow from you. You have a renewed spirit within your soul.

Awake, O north wind; and come, thou south; blow upon my garden, that the spices thereof may flow out. Let my beloved come into his garden, and eat his pleasant fruits. (4:16)
You are willing to be broken by the harsh north winds experience, yet still your fragrance flows out of you ministering to others. In your brokenness you still bear fruit sweet to my taste.

The one thing I have always desired since I first came to know the Lord was to know His voice, His thoughts and His feelings. So how come when they apply to me, I don't really believe it? Sounds good that He is talking about me but I know me. I knew my biggest problem I needed overcome was to actually believe all this about myself. How do I see myself as He sees me?

He gave me the answer in Matt 22:39 And the second is like it: 'You shall love your neighbor as yourself.'

How do you learn to love yourself? Love in this scripture is agapaō or to love, to be of good will and exhibit the same, to have preference to, wish well to, regard the welfare of. For the word yourself, Webster's uses a definition that I like....your true normal self. I had to ask myself when I take off my mask, my covered up identity; do I love what I see? Do I love the fact that God is working in my life making me more like Him, than what I see negative in the physical?

How could I put my heart into something and leave myself out of it? It's impossible. By being the unique wonderful person God created me to be and accepting myself with all the faults I see, would give me a simple peace within that would make others around me happy also.

It was a really hard thing, even scary, to accept myself completely. I think many times I am my own worst enemy. God loves me so much, what made me think that I did not deserve my own love?

I wondered if I had become jealous of the time I had spent learning to love other people because I had not taken any time for loving myself. I believe that making a decision to love myself was a decision to want to come to a fuller life than I have ever experienced. I had to believe that I am unique and not a mistake. God does not make mistakes! He created me for a purpose and I am perfect for that. I have great value in the kingdom and nothing can change that!

I am not talking about pride here but a genuine happiness and acceptance in the beauty that God has created in me. There are many areas in my life that did not come into the picture here. Who I was on the inside is the important thing, not what I did for a living or how I looked. God has put something so special inside of me, just for you because He loves me.

Look again at the meaning of the word love. To love, to be of good will and exhibit the same, to have preference to, wish well to, regard the welfare of. Did I show myself the same preference and regard my welfare as much as others? I was thinking perhaps I should practice this a little more in my life. God was showing me that my opinion and thoughts did matter to him. I am not talking about being selfish but considerate about your own self. He loves me; shouldn't I learn to love myself? Love the things of this world that He loves....me.

I wish I knew a one, two, three plan to give you on how to love yourself but I can't. Ask God to show you how to accomplish this.

He is so faithful and loves you enough to show you. We each have our own path to follow and he is the only one who knows yours all the way to the last step.

I had so much to learn. I found myself still trying to earn His love because I could not believe what he had just said to me. I struggled with becoming a perfectionist. If it wasn't perfect it made me angry and frustrated. I could have easily worked myself to death trying to keep a super clean house, raise two kids and still work full time (all the time doing drugs so I could handle it all). This caused me to battle to delegate because I felt if others or I did not do the job well enough, I would be rejected.

"Both you and these people who are with you will surely wear yourselves out. For this thing is too much for you; you are not able to perform it by yourself. Listen now to my voice; I will give you counsel and God will be with you: Stand before God for the people, so that you may bring the difficulties to God." Exodus 18:18-19

It is wonderful now that I can find my identity in Christ and not in what I can achieve. I was not great at achieving all I expected of myself. Ok, now I can begin to really hear what he had to say about me but I wondered what else is keeping me from fully hearing? How much more of the cold north winds can I handle? Will the warm rain and gentle winds keep coming after the harsh brokenness of the north wind hit me again? Do I love myself and Him enough to keep going?

Chapter 6
Frantic Pursuit

I am come into my garden, my sister, my spouse: I have gathered my myrrh with my spice; I have eaten my honeycomb with my honey; I have drunk my wine with my milk: eat, O friends; drink, yea, drink abundantly, O beloved. (5:1)

He was reassuring me that I was his garden but He calls me not only His sister but also His spouse. I thought about this, experiences which siblings experience together belong to them alone, along with flesh and blood. The same as husband and wife share experiences that belong only to them. Here is He telling me that I have a fullness of experiences with him. He has been with me as I have matured and I share His flesh and blood but now I am with Him as His spouse. He was telling me about His life, the struggles and the good times and bad times. He did it all for me.

Suddenly I began to see it differently, He had been talking of His life, yet He lives in me and now He is talking about me. Those were my struggles, my good times and bad and now He was going to share the fruit of all of this with others. He reminded me that I am a garden sealed for Him. That meant private and it was up to Him to choose who would be able to partake of my fruit. I must listen and only give as He directs because I am His. He said to me, "Not everything in your life is to be shared with just anyone. Remember it is I who asked you to dance. It is I who leads the dance. If you follow my lead...No toes will be stepped on...No steps will be missed. The dance will flow freely only if you follow My lead!"

How scary it is to have parts of your life exposed for others to see. I still could not believe I would have something of value that others would want. I spent too much time comparing myself to others around me.

Wish I could quote scriptures like that, wish I had that much wisdom and on and on. Didn't He just tell me that I was perfectly equipped for what he had for me to do in this life?

I sleep, but my heart waketh: it is the voice of my beloved that knocketh, saying, Open to me, my sister, my love, my dove, my undefiled: for my head is filled with dew, and my locks with the drops of the night. (5: 2)

I am not always quick to jump to action. I will stand back and analyze what is before me. Many times I would rather not deal with whatever it is, as if it would just go away if I ignored it. I was troubled in my spirit, I had found a place of rest and yet I could hear the knock, bidding me to arise. I tried to rest but the stories keep coming to my mind. I thought of the story of His disciples, who could not stay awake just one hour while Jesus prayed. When they awoke, the soldiers came to take Jesus away and they were never with Him in the same way again. The ten virgins who slumbered and then are awakened at the sound of the bridegroom coming and not all were ready. Would I have enough oil? What exactly is this oil?

You see some came with only their lamps; some came with their lamps and additional oil. Each came with a lamp with some oil in it. Oil was one of the most valuable commodities at that time and it is still true. That oil represents the Holy Spirit or intimacy with God. The lamp could represent your life or your ministry depending on where your heart is. Some came to say, "Look at me, look at what I am doing". Many will say to me on that day, 'Lord, Lord, did we not prophesy in your name and in your name drive out demons and perform many miracles?' Then I will tell them plainly, "I never knew you. Away from me, you evildoers!" Matt 7:22-23

In the time that story was written the use of oil was a sign of gladness and the omission of it represented sorrow. I think the story says more than we realize.

The first commandment says to love your God with all your heart, or shall I put it this way, obtain extra oil! The very thing that we are to obtain is what we will be judged by. See the foolish brought only enough oil to shine for the moment, to make a show as if they were to meet the bridegroom right away, if they had only had the intimacy to know his heart.

Intimacy only comes from an innermost, very personal, private relationship. No one can give you his or her oil. They both had one common fault they all fell asleep. We are all human. All the virgins were the same at that moment until that final cry came, "The bridegroom is coming!" The foolish ones said, "Oh, our lamps are going out." And they realized at that time that they didn't have the true light, but it was also at that time too late. Romans 8:9 says And if anyone does not have the Spirit of Christ, he does not belong to Christ. We have the Holy Spirit to help us obtain more oil, if we will only listen.

As I pondered all this, the truth in my mind was I felt if I got up, I would not measure up. I would not have enough light to make a difference. I wanted to just rest but somehow my heart had come into tune with His voice. "Why is He calling me all those wonderful things? He must know that I am tarrying, hesitant to get up." What was happening was that He was trying to get me to go to place where I could obtain more oil. I wondered how many times had he patiently knocked at my heart's door only to find me asleep, yet he waited for me to make up my mind. It is not always in the restful and beautiful places that I would hear His voice. I was in a hard place in my life and yet I heard His voice, now I must awaken enough to respond.

How long must you stand outside to have your head become heavy with dew? I don't believe I would have that much patience but my Jesus does.

How could I be so cruel to Him and tarry? Why couldn't I have jumped up immediately and said, "Yes, Lord here I come!"   Then the thought came why doesn't He, the bridegroom, have a key?

I have put off my coat; how shall I put it on? I have washed my feet; how shall I defile them? (5:3)
I found myself making excuses again. Why I couldn't answer His call? I was thinking things are finally working well at home and my family now needs me. I am working 2 part time jobs so I am tired. I thought if I came out a little farther with him, all those things of my past would come back at me for one last shot. Maybe I would not be able to handle all this. Couldn't He see this is just too much for me? Isn't it enough that I have already taken off that old life? It would be better to wait a little while until I was sure I could handle things without reverting to my old way.

Isn't it enough that I have been washed clean from my former sins and choose to live for Him? Where was my trust in Him? All my own troubles and thoughts seemed to be clouding my mind, my judgment and I was growing closer to being asleep. I couldn't see that He was trying to move me into a place where he could do something for me. I couldn't see past the place I was at. The only thing I could see was that to answer that door it would require me to get up 'barefooted' where I would be able to feel anything I stepped on. I could only see possible pain. Being in a state of having my emotions starting to open up was a very threatening thought for me.

There was a price for wanting things on my own terms. The bridegroom was calling me to dance and I was trying to take the lead. There is more to the cross than salvation and turning from your old ways. There is the resurrection power that he was calling me into.

It was a whole new life that He was calling me out to. It would be a life full of emotion and the fullness of life. I pulled back into my old ways and drew back to safety.

My beloved put in his hand by the hole of the door, and my bowels were moved for him. (5:4)
Somehow I knew that He would be dealing with my refusal to come out. What had I done? Is it a sin to not come right away when called? I knew He could have come in and pulled me out but it had to be my choice. I watched to see what he would do. He put his hand to the hole in the latch.
Would he open the latch to my heart? Then I saw it, the nail scar in his hand. This moved my heart more than I can tell you. I have a huge scar on my hand and only a few know the truth of how it got there and the pain that was in my heart that day. As I looked at his hand, I knew the pain that I had felt in my heart was so small compared to the pain He felt on that day. I realized that he had given me the key and somehow I had locked the door. Just that gentle stretched out hand had awakened my heart. How could I have been so selfish? I must put on the robe of humility and open the door!

I rose up to open to my beloved; and my hands dropped with myrrh, and my fingers with sweet smelling myrrh, upon the handles of the lock. (5:5)
So I decided to open the door. What that really meant was that I had decided to open my heart back up to him. You can cry out to him all you want but as long as you keep that locked door in your heart, He will not break it down. You have to choose to open up to Him. This was requiring more of me than to just lie in rest and wishing that He would come in.

As I was thinking on this, in a moment, I standing within my heart with the presence of the Holy Spirit so strong, I could not believe I was still standing.

(When you feel the Holy Spirit outside your body, it doesn't compare to the presence in your heart.) I saw all these closed doors. I asked, "What are these doors? Where do they go? Why are they closed?" The answer I received was "These are rooms of darkness, they lead to death and you have allowed them to remain here untouched. It is up to you to open the doors and allow the light to overcome the darkness." I was so surprised at the number of closed doors there were. They no longer had any place here. So I opened a door. As soon as I did the light of the Holy Spirit rushed in and overcame the darkness. The light inside my heart increased. The room to which I had opened the door, in a split second was gone. It no longer existed. The open area in which the Holy Spirit was dwelling increased in size. It was as if the room had never been there, there was no trace of it left.

That looked easy, just open the door, but somehow I knew it was not quite that simple. I looked at my hands, myrrh dripped from my hands. In opening this door, I am choosing to walk into his death, which meant more death to my flesh. So many things were running through my mind.

Just what am I really giving up? Flashes of past pains and sorrow flooded my mind. The pain seemed more than I could bear. Why would I want to choose to continue to live with all this?

I opened to my beloved; but my beloved had withdrawn himself, and was gone: my soul failed when he spake: I sought him, but I could not find him; I called him, but he gave me no answer. (5:6)

I knew that when it came down to it, I would have to be the one to open the door. I somehow just wanted Him to break down the door and rescue me.

I now realized the truth of being the only one who could open the door. My Lord would never force himself upon me; it had to be my choice. I just could not lie and rest anymore and wish He would come in and possess my heart.

I thought I knew Him, but now I realize that I do not really know much about him. How many times have we bragged that we know God, yet we do not throw open the door to everything we are and let Him have His way in our lives without any hindrance from our flesh? In order to possess us to the fullest, He must move into every part of our being. This action took faith in the fact that He is love. He wants me more than I want Him and He is willing to do whatever it takes to draw me out.

When I was sleeping, He knocked; while I stubbornly refused to get up, He called; but when He finally aroused my heart enough to open the door, then He turned and is gone. Simply I think, "What?" As I think about it, He offered his best and I hesitated to open up. I heard His voice, I recognized His presence at the door, yet I rationalized the practicality of getting up. God is so loving and amazing; I now see that by turning away, He is telling me that my response was not good enough. He wants the best for me. He is drawing me out of myself to a deeper level. This self-indulgence and indifference will never do for His bride.

So the search begins. I must find Him but somehow I can't. It is becoming frantic in my heart. "How do I change this choice I have made?" I call and it seems that He does not hear me but deep inside I know that He does.

My first thoughts are "He doesn't really care. Is this really worth it?" and "I am much better now than before, so why go any farther."

I am battling my flesh right now. Who will I choose to serve; myself or the only One who only wants me to have the fullness of life? I have chosen fullness; so my frantic search begins.

The watchmen that went about the city found me, they smote me, they wounded me; the keepers of the walls took away my veil from me. (5:7)

I learned something very interesting about the body of Christ; if one person becomes frantic in their search; it begins to bother the flock. I think because I was hungrier than they were, it seemed that some wanted to find a way to stop me. I cannot say what triggers this reaction in people except sometimes when we see a lack in our lives, we try to justify the comfortable place we are at, by basically attacking the one who is in frantic pursuit.

I experienced some of those in leadership coming to me with the complaints of others in the body. They were saying, "If she only did this or that." In doing this they were justifying their own comfortable place on the pew. I was so blessed to have a pastor who did not fall into their trap.

They were opening up all my problems, it seemed, to the whole church with their complaining and talking between each other. This I could say was a spiritual wounding, until the Lord showed me that it was not the Romans who came to seize Jesus.

And while He was still speaking, behold, Judas, one of the twelve, with a great multitude with swords and clubs, came from the chief priests and elders of the people. Matt 26:47

It was as if they resented my hunger and my great need to repent and change my life, just as the chief priests and elders had resented Jesus for listening to His father and not following their religious rules. It was as if they wanted me to keep quiet and slip back into sleep. They were happy and satisfied with where they were. Why would they want more of Him? What they were really accomplishing was revealing their own hearts but they were blind to it.

I had to decide what I wanted in life, the approval of the flock or to know the only One who was healing me and had everything I needed. The words of what they thought I should do were merely a compromise to make them feel better about themselves. I just could not compromise to make them happy.

What happened next was amazing. The veil was ripped from my eyes and I was able to see the Lord in a depth that was not possible before. I had a slight understanding of the pain He suffered. I guess there is nothing that could have fired up the pursuit in me more than persecution. I felt my passion firing up even more.

Many of you say, "Isn't it enough that I have put off my old nature and way of life?" I say, Come in deeper, bare your feet! Without shoes, your feet become more sensitive. Every pebble, every thorn, every rock can be felt. Things you did not feel before, you will now feel. You will share in My sufferings.

I charge you, O daughters of Jerusalem, if ye find my beloved, that ye tell him, that I am sick of love. (5:8)

When the Lord pulls you into a place so close to him, it seems like no one else could ever know what you know.

This is true to a small degree, His intimacy with you is just for you and made for you, but he is intimate with all of His beloved who would choose it. It is just different but the same, specially tailored to the needs of the beloved. I had come to the humbling fact that I was not the only one and someone else could maybe find him before I did. I was just frantic enough to not want to miss any chance to regain His presence that I would ask for help.

I am sure Satan meant for this to pull me away from my bridegroom to stop my pursuit. I still loved Jesus; even though it seemed He had gone. If my love had been halfhearted or if I was backslidden, I would not still feel the ties of love that still bound us together. I was beginning to understand something I had never known in my life.

Love suffers long and is kind; love does not envy; love does not parade itself, is not puffed up; does not behave rudely, does not seek its own, is not provoked, thinks no evil; does not rejoice in iniquity, but rejoices in the truth; bears all things, believes all things, hopes all things, endures all things. Love never fails. But whether there are prophecies, they will fail; whether there are tongues, they will cease; whether there is knowledge, it will vanish away. I Cor 13: 4-8

I felt a bit like Job but he loved God or why would have he said, "Though He slay me, yet will I trust Him. Even so, I will defend my own ways before Him."

I had such a longing and need for him that I was 'sick with love'. Before I was 'sick with love' because it had seemed I could not handle any more of his sweet love. This was so different, such a hurt, a longing and the separation seemed unbearable.

The pain seemed so much deeper than anything I had experienced in the physical. How could this be possible? I had never felt such pain in my heart before. Is this divine love?

What is thy beloved more than another beloved, O thou fairest among women? what is thy beloved more than another beloved, that thou dost so charge us? (5:9)
I was so amazed at what happened next. As I began to ask others in the body about how to find Him again and share the love sickness in my heart, I was surprised by the response I got from some. These are ones who I respected and I had just assumed they would surely be more 'spiritual' than me. They began to question me as if the One I knew was somehow different than the One they knew. I guess the consuming hunger in my heart was speaking louder than my words. I could hardly believe that my hunger was stirring something within their hearts.

They were aware of the things that had been said about "what I should do"; and yet this timid scared person was moving forward overcoming the former fear of man I had that had been so evident to all. Suddenly it was me sharing the sweet love of God I had experienced and they were consuming every word. I had decided in my heart many years before as a child that I would never reveal my heart openly again because of the repercussions I had experienced. I was like Jeremiah who tried to hold the word of God back from his mouth but could not.

Then I said, "I will not make mention of Him, nor speak anymore in His name." But His word was in my heart like a burning fire shut up in my bones; I was weary of holding it back, And I could not. Jer 20:9

I was totally absorbed in the pursuit and all my walls were falling down, without me even realizing it. This divine love was changing me and I had no power to keep those walls up.

My beloved is white and ruddy, the chiefest among ten thousand. (5:10)
As I began to share, the zeal for divine love began to burn hotter. The more I shared of the limited knowledge I had of him; the more my heart was quicken to find Him once more.

I could not help but to share about the beauty and incredible appearance of the one I had found. He was the brightest and clearest light I have ever experienced; yet, He was still willing to die, to be slain, just for me. How could someone, so pure, lay down His life willingly for such a sinner as me? The two colors together fit perfectly together to put a desire in me to become His bride. This was His new covenant to me, His bride. He was dazzling white yet the red was showing through. He was clothing me in His righteousness. I could not really prepare myself to be His bride; it was He who was preparing me. I just needed to submit to the preparation.

"Let us be glad and rejoice and give Him glory, for the marriage of the Lamb has come, and His wife has made herself ready." Rev 19:7

He was my new standard. The original word in this verse was 'chiefest' which meant a banner or standard. Ten thousand did not mean what we consider that particular number but an infinite number. There never has or never will be a banner or standard over my life which could even come close to Him. He brought me to the banqueting house, and his banner over me was love. Song 2:4

His head is as the most fine gold, his locks are bushy, and black as a raven. (5:11)
God is the head of the church and the head of my life. He is the supreme divine authority! One thing I know for sure is the curly, bushy hair is strong. I have curly hair and it keeps its shape, it doesn't droop or fall. Black as a raven refers to the youthfulness of the Lord, he will never grow old.

Jesus Christ is the same yesterday, today, and forever. Hebrew 13:8

His eyes are as the eyes of doves by the rivers of waters, washed with milk, and fitly set. (5:12)
I can see that His eyes are fixed directly on me, He has that single vision that a dove has, mated to me for life. He will never give up on me. His eyes that are fixed on me are gentle and peaceful. Although He can have fire in His eyes; these are not the eyes I see looking at me. They give me strength, just as milk gives strength to the weak. This keeps me young in His sight.

His cheeks are as a bed of spices, as sweet flowers: his lips like lilies, dropping sweet smelling myrrh (5:13)
His cheeks are as the seat of sweetness and beauty. Our cheeks often show our emotions, the emotions of my Jesus are the sweetest smelling fragrances to me.

The love, the passion and the pouring out of His life produce sweet incenses like no other. His lips are like no other so pure, delicate with a sweet smell, yet the gently and sweetly urging me on to death of my flesh. Myrrh also has a wonderful healing quality to it.

"It is the Spirit who gives life; the flesh profits nothing. The words that I speak to you are spirit, and they are life." John 6:63

As His sweet Spirit would speak to my heart ever so softly and gently, it seemed to lay my heart bare. I would have it no other way. He can speak anything He wants to me and I will treasure it.

For the word of God is living and powerful, and sharper than any two-edged sword, piercing even to the division of soul and spirit, and of joints and marrow, and is a discerner of the thoughts and intents of the heart. Heb 4:12

His hands are as gold rings set with the beryl: his belly is as bright ivory overlaid with sapphires. (5:14)
His hands were working out His will for my life. After being exposed to His divine nature, I was beginning to give Him the authority to rule in my life. He had always had the authority but He had waited ever so gently until I was ready to recognize that authority in my life. His will and authority are set in beryl which is found as the eight stones in the new city in Revelation 21:20. The number eight generally symbolizes resurrection. The stone is green which symbolizes freshness, vigor and new life.

I am beginning to see how from His hands the resurrection of my life flows. In His body, His Heart I can see that which is bright, polished and precious. It takes great skill to carve ivory and inlay it with sapphires. Sapphires are blue which represents the presence of God. Can you see the beauty of it?

His legs are as pillars of marble, set upon sockets of fine gold: his countenance is as Lebanon, excellent as the cedars. (5:15)
I had to have someone strong in my life. Someone who would stand strong for me with the finest character; this is what My bridegroom was becoming to me. Looking upon Him was like looking at the most beautiful mountain range....majestic, no other like Him. He is the King of all kings and even the best of this world cannot compare to Him.

His mouth is most sweet: yea, he is altogether lovely. This is my beloved, and this is my friend, O daughters of Jerusalem. (5:16)
Everything He said to me, even if it seemed hard, was sweet to me. I would not change one thing! A friend is someone who is close enough to speak into your life honestly because they care about you. I realized I had found the friend that I had searched for my entire life.

A man who has friends must himself be friendly, But there is a friend who sticks closer than a brother. Prov 18:24

And the Scripture was fulfilled which says, "Abraham believed God, and it was accounted to him for righteousness." And he was called the friend of God. James 2:23

Chapter 7
My Love Overwhelms His Heart

Whither is thy beloved gone, O thou fairest among women? whither is thy beloved turned aside? that we may seek him with thee. (6:1)

The more I began to describe this love, this friend I had found; it seemed the more others began to ask questions. I thought about it and I realized that the people I knew who were just going through the motions of loving God really did not draw me. The ones that sparked my interest had been ones whose passion was so evident to all.

It was not all the things that I had experienced with God that made others want to join in with my search; it was the passion that I had, that made them want to seek Him. People who live off others experiences never seem to want to seek out an experience for themselves. This is sad but true. People are natural followers unless it takes them out their comfort zone, then they seem content to just stay where they are.

Whom have I in heaven but You? And there is none upon earth that I desire besides You. Psalm 73:25

I think up to this point in my life I had been just that lady with a whole lot of hurt in her life to the others in the church. Now the change in my life was becoming evident to those around me. I was beginning to believe that others could actually see Jesus in me! I had to come to the realization deep in my heart that He really was all I did desire. I seemed to have a deeper reality of His presence. Even after all I had experienced with Him; this was deeper than I had ever experienced and I was not laying on the floor in His presence. I was just sharing my love for Him with others. This was the high of all highs! Then suddenly, I saw where he had gone.

My beloved is gone down into his garden, to the beds of spices, to feed in the gardens, and to gather lilies. (6:2)
This is the intimacy I had always desired. I suddenly understood that I am His garden and He does dwell inside of me. He was not just that sweet voice, the electricity that swept over me time after time for the last five years; even though these are very precious to me, this was much greater! He had really been more of a visitor before. Now he had become a part of me or I should say I had become a part of him. Somehow in this healing process that I had gone through, I had learned to share in his sufferings. My focus had shifted off my hurts and this world to Him.

For I consider that the sufferings of this present time are not worthy to be compared with the glory which shall be revealed in us. Romans 8:18

Now faith is the substance of things hoped for, the evidence of things not seen. Hebrews 11:1

He had become my hope and everything important to me. I had the faith to know that as His garden he would never leave me and would always care for me. God gave me a vision of how he had cared for me through this cleansing I had been going through and why he had such a purpose in it all.

I saw a bottle split out on the ground. Black, sticky, smelly ooze was flowing out of it. People walked by and looked at it with disgust, saying things like..."Someone ought to clean that up"...."I wouldn't touch that sticky mess, someone else will have to clean it up"..."That should not be HERE"..Etc.
Then the Lord passed by wearing a beautiful white robe. He knelt beside the bottle and the ooze with tears in his eyes. He had found something so precious; it touched his heart so much that it brought tears to his eyes.

He lay down on top of the whole mess, covering it with his body. As he stood up, he had a black stain from the ooze on his white robe. He had soaked if off the ground onto himself. As I watched, the stain soon disappeared and the robe became white again. Then he held up the bottle. It had become beautiful, sparkling clean with fresh water bubbling up out of it. He said, "Because the bottle was willing to let the black flow out of it and to be shamed by man because of what needed to come out...I have made it a vessel of honor!"

I am my beloved's, and my beloved is mine: he feedeth among the lilies. (6:3)
I decided to give myself completely to Him. I was not sure how you would go about doing this; but this is my decision. I will just listen and do what he tells me to do. This will be my place to start. I know now that no matter what life throws at me, he will be with me.

I never really saw or understood before but he has always been with me. I have finally found the peace and true rest I have desired. This is not based on feelings but a growing trust and faith in Him.

For most of my life, I had gotten up several times a night and checked the house, checked the kids, just making sure everything was ok. This uneasiness came from the years of abuse and the fear you live in. Suddenly I just started sleeping peacefully through the night. It scared me at first because the fear of 'something happened' while I slept came upon me. The peace of God inside of me was much greater than the fear and it had to leave. The Lord has our future as his pure spotless bride in his thoughts. We are His desire.

Isaiah 43:1b-2..."Fear not, for I have redeemed you, I have called you by your name; you are mine. When you pass through the waters, I will be with you; And through the rivers, they will not overflow you. When you walk through the fire, you shall not be burned, nor shall the flame scorch you."

Thou art beautiful, O my love, as Tirzah, comely as Jerusalem, terrible as an army with banners. (6:4)
Suddenly I was hearing his voice clearly again! He began telling me how beautiful I was and pleasing. He was comparing me to his beautiful city with His love as my banner. Things were not going well at home that day and I was feeling a bit discouraged even with all this encouragement. Sometimes I let my situations get on top of me, when I should be on top of the situations. But God loves me so much and would not let me remain in a place of discouragement. He knew just what I needed. I was trying in my own strength to change my thoughts. Sometimes just like looking at old photos, it does the heart good to put on an old worship song from years ago and remember the wonderful things God spoke to me at that time. I tried that and then I headed off to the safest place I knew, my church. Then during worship I heard the Lord singing.

There is no way to describe the passion I heard. You need to hear Him sing for yourself. No one sings like the Lord.
We were singing a song called 'Here I am to worship', which has a line that says "I'll never know how much it cost, to see my sin upon that cross." As I sang I pondered on the reality of that line, I heard the Lord speak to me. He said, "You will never know how much it cost but that cost is my wedding gift to you." Then He began to sing....

"So here I am to love you, Here I am to hold you, Here I am to say that you're My bride. You're altogether lovely, Altogether worthy, Altogether wonderful to Me. You'll never know how much it cost to see your sin upon My cross. So here I am to love you......."

The next evening I came to church feeling hurt and a bit beat up by something someone had done to me. Then the Lord began to sing sweetly into my heart again. This time He changed just one word but it changed my whole attitude. He sang...

"You'll never know how much it cost to feel your sin upon My cross. So here I am to love you, Here I am to hold you, Here I am to say that you' you're My bride."

My hurt feelings just faded away. God's love is greater than we could ever imagine!

Isaiah 62:5b..."as a bridegroom rejoices over his bride, so will your God rejoice over you."

Turn away thine eyes from me, for they have overcome me: thy hair is as a flock of goats that appear from Gilead (6:5)
This is not rejection; He is overcome with the love of the bride for Him. He was saying to me, "Your love overwhelms My heart!" I do not ever want to lose that desire for the Lord. I want Him to see this love every time He looks in my eyes. The Lord tests us over and over again to reveal our hearts. Do we love Him for Himself alone?

I have seen Jesus smile at me several times in my life. One time as a child, I was hurt and cold, hiding in some bushes next to the sanctuary of the church we lived next to.

I remember looking at Jesus on the cross through the window. I thought he must have felt as I did. He looked down from that cross directly at me and smiled. Although I didn't know who He was, I never forgot that smile. I wonder now, what did he see in my eyes?....my longing for Him....a Savior?

A few years ago I saw Him smile at me again. I was in the sanctuary of my church allowing Him to wash away a lifetime of hurt from my life. I wonder, what did he see in my eyes then?....my need for Him...a Healer?

The eyes are said to be the window to the soul. They reveal the heart. When I was immature and Jesus looked upon my eyes and saw my heart, I never realized that I could overwhelm Him with my love. I knew that just the love in His smile could overwhelm me. Since we are created in His image it only makes sense that we could return that same love to Him. I feel the Lord has a great longing in His heart to be overwhelmed with the love of His people. Just as the bridegroom longs for His bride before the wedding, the Lord longs for us.

We need to return to our first love. My desire is that my love would continue to grow so strong that when my Lord looks into my eyes, His heart would be moved by my pure love for Him. Do your eyes move the heart of God? What does He see in your eyes now?....deep, strong love....as a bride for her groom. He continued speaking to me saying, "I see great strength in your strong love. Because your love is so strong and you have separated yourself from the hurts of the past, I will be your strength in this world and for eternity."

Thy teeth are as a flock of sheep which go up from the washing, whereof every one beareth twins, and there is not one barren among them. (6:6)

I somehow knew that I was truly becoming the things he was telling me I was. This was not a future description of what I would be as before; but a description of how I was changing, how my mind was being renewed. I was able now to consume his word and eagerly dig into it at a deeper level. When things came against me, I was now turning to the word to find comfort and revelation. The things that the worldly counselors and books were saying about people who lived through pains similar to mine no longer applied to me. I had found a balance in my life, yet I was not willing to stop there. There was so much truth and wisdom to be found in His word. I wanted God's will for my life to be done.

As a piece of a pomegranate are thy temples within thy locks. (7:7)
I may be able to hide my feelings from the world but I could no longer deny Him access to any part of me. His thoughts were becoming my thoughts. I could see the depth at which He had worked in my life.

Instead of doing like some and blurting out all the things He was sharing with me, I will wait until He tells me to share and only what He wants me to share. I was always intimidated by those "more spiritual than me" people who talked like no one ever talked to them except God himself. There is a balance. I am not sure if it was just pride or not really knowing who they are in Christ that makes them put on the air of being superior when they see others fail to line up to the mark. I am satisfied to simply know He loves me and He is the one I wish to please.

There are threescore queens, and fourscore concubines, and virgins without number. My dove, my undefiled is but one; she is the only one of her mother, she is the choice one of her that bare her. The daughters saw her, and blessed her; yea, the queens and the concubines, and they praised her. (7:8-9)

It seems to me that many do not understand there are a multitude of people who are good and have knowledge about God and some even do great things but there is only one perfect prepared bride. The tongue can speak many things but there is only one perfect unity of hearts. That perfect unity is between the heart of the bridegroom and the bride. Great words and works will all pass away; the passion of love is eternal. They may seem to gain status in the church and among believers but my heart aches for them because of the love they do not understand.

Love never fails. But whether there are prophecies, they will fail; whether there are tongues, they will cease; whether there is knowledge, it will vanish away. 1 Cor 13:8

I really felt that God was telling me that someday the others in the church would appreciate the passion I had. It was not that I needed their approval but I knew they were missing out. When I was in the world and I had a good drug, I wanted to share it with my friends to enjoy also.

And we know that all things work together for good to those who love God, to those who are the called according to His purpose. Romans 8:28

Who is she that looketh forth as the morning, fair as the moon, clear as the sun, and terrible as an army with banners? (6:10)

I was becoming like Jesus. Isaiah prophesied about Jesus in Matthew 4:16-17 it came to be....the people living in darkness have seen a light; on those living in the land of the shadow of death a light has dawned. Others were beginning to see a light in me that had never been there before. Not all could understand but many knew that this was a supernatural light and recognized that I was becoming a reflection of my sweet Lord.

But the path of the just is like the shining sun, That shines ever brighter unto the perfect day. Prov 4:18

God spoke to me and told me that I was like the woman found in Luke with the issue of blood. But Jesus said, "Somebody touched Me, for I perceived power going out from Me." Now when the woman saw that she was not hidden, she came trembling; and falling down before Him, she declared to Him in the presence of all the people the reason she had touched Him and how she was healed immediately. And He said to her, "Daughter, be of good cheer; your faith has made you well. Go in peace." Luke 8:46-48

He said to me, "In the large crowd she was in, when I spoke, why did she know she was not hidden? The answer is simply, she knew and understood in her heart that I am. Once the power went out of me to her, she was not only healed but the glory of God was visible for all to see. This is what has happened to you, you will no longer be able to hide from my people. They will be drawn to you, for it is my light in you, which is drawing them. The faith you have in Me will always be enough for you, never forget this."

From a woman who was identified only by hurt of the past, like the woman with an issue of blood, I had become a whole creature, named and identified with Jesus -- from broken to a delivered bride. What a wonderful change in my life simply by touching Jesus. These truths were not just for me but for all that are becoming his bride!

But we all, with unveiled face, beholding as in a mirror the glory of the Lord, are being transformed into the same image from glory to glory, just as by the Spirit of the Lord. 2 Cor 3:18

I was not only becoming the bride but a part of the army here on earth. Flying high the banners of love and worship for the only One and Holy King!

I went down into the garden of nuts to see the fruits of the valley, and to see whether the vine flourished, and the pomegranates budded. (7:11)
I was beginning to see things differently, as I started to look again at the promises God had spoken into my life, I began to ask for Him to reveal what the real meaning was. A nut has to be broken to reveal the meat inside.

But the natural man does not receive the things of the Spirit of God, for they are foolishness to him; nor can he know them, because they are spiritually discerned. 1 Cor 2:14

I could see that the fruit in my life had begun developing in the low places, the valleys of my life. Now I could begin to look at others in low places and see the beauty that was beginning to develop there also.   He was sending me out to tend a portion of his vineyard! This was so excited, yet scary, because even with all this happening it was still a new place for me. I did not know how to minister to others so I decided that I could pray and intercede for them.

Or ever I was aware, my soul made me like the chariots of Amminadib. (6:12)
As I prayed, I began to be swept up into a realm that I had never experienced before. This was a greater level of His presence than I had ever experienced. I was taken to Heaven on several occasions so God could show me some things that are truths in the spirit realm but may not make sense to this world. He was teaching me His ways. I did not want to leave this place I was in, but how could His will in my life be fulfilled if I stayed?

He showed me how He looks at the heart of worship in His people. He showed me my home in heaven and it really didn't fit what others had described but then again, they are not me. He spoke to me about the right time to share things he was showing me and to discern who to share with.

Return, return, O Shulamite; return, return, that we may look upon thee. What will ye see in the Shulamite? As it were the company of two armies. (6:13)
My friends were not sure what had exactly happened to me, but they knew there was now a separation had taken place. This was not a physical separation but in the Spirit I was going places they could not understand. I didn't care about things like shopping anymore which was something we did together. I only wanted to go to the sanctuary to pray and meet with God. I spent hours in the sanctuary. The experiences I had during these prayer times were absolutely incredible and very personal.

I was beginning to take on His name. How do I know this? Shulimite is the feminine form of Solomon or one made peaceful. Through all the pain and torment in my life, I had somehow been made peaceful. Peace lives in my heart now, the exact opposite of how I use to live. It was time to go out.

Too many say, "What can the church have for the world to look at?" The dance was called the dance of two camps. These two camps was the place where Jacob was met by the angels of God. Many say, "What would the world see in me? It's not about us. It's about the spirit that dwells within us.

Each time I think, "What could I have to offer?" God reminds me of the woman with the issue of blood and it is the Glory of God from the power that flows out of me because of who is in me that I have something to offer.

I am just the vessel; that is my offering to the world. I am to be like Him, His reflection to the world.

"Heal the sick, cleanse the lepers, raise the dead, cast out demons. Freely you have received, freely give." Matt 10:8

"No one, when he has lit a lamp, covers it with a vessel or puts it under a bed, but sets it on a lampstand, that those who enter may see the light." Luke 8:16

Nevertheless the solid foundation of God stands, having this seal: "The Lord knows those who are His," and, "Let everyone who names the name of Christ depart from iniquity." But in a great house there are not only vessels of gold and silver, but also of wood and clay, some for honor and some for dishonor. Therefore if anyone cleanses himself from the latter, he will be a vessel for honor, sanctified and useful for the Master, prepared for every good work. 2 Tim 2:19-21

Chapter 8
His Delight & Going Out

How beautiful are thy feet with shoes, O prince's daughter! the joints of thy thighs are like jewels, the work of the hands of a cunning workman. (7:1)
My feet were no longer bare. People could see a difference as I walked. An authority that was never there before came upon me. I was beginning to know who I am and what my true heritage is. I am a child of the King but also His bride!

And how shall they preach unless they are sent? As it is written: "How beautiful are the feet of those who preach the gospel of peace, who bring glad tidings of good things!" Romans 10:15

In the physical the thighs give you strength to walk and run. I had the opportunity to go to Brownsville, FL during the renewal in the 90's. I had the most unique experience there. It was a miracle I ended up there because I was really had a fear of driving and I was in New Orleans at an Aglow conference. There were many things that happened on that trip but my passion to get more of God overrode my fears. I rented a car and took some friends and off we went to meet with God.

I had made up my mind that I would not leave until I had received everything that God had for me. I ran up when asked, "Who wants more of God?" Once again I found myself on the floor in his presence. Finally someone lifted me off the floor and escorted me to the door; they needed to clean the church. "How long had I been there?"

I love my friends! They were waiting outside next to the car. I had the keys to the rental car in my pocket and all our purses were locked in the trunk. That was love in action, they were happy to wait for me.

We got in the car and I was going to drive. As I went to put the keys in the ignition, I noticed this heat radiating from my thighs. I made everyone in the car confirm this. It lasted for quite some time. At the time, I was not sure what the purpose was for that radiating heat was. I know now that God was showing me that He had given me supernatural strength to walk through some of the places of life I had to walk through.

A jewel is one that is highly esteemed. God is the ultimate skilled workman. He will work on your life and character until you resemble his Son. The truth of God in our lives will make us sparkle as jewels, in this world, designed and crafted by God himself. We are not esteemed by who we are but by who lives in us!

For wisdom is better than rubies, And all the things one may desire cannot be compared with her. Prov 8:11

There is gold and a multitude of rubies, But the lips of knowledge are a precious jewel. Prov 20:15

A Psalm. A Song at the dedication of the house of David. I will extol You, O LORD, for You have lifted me up, And have not let my foes rejoice over me. O LORD my God, I cried out to You, And You healed me. O LORD, You brought my soul up from the grave; You have kept me alive, that I should not go down to the pit. Sing praise to the LORD, you saints of His, And give thanks at the remembrance of His holy name. For His anger is but for a moment, His favor is for life; Weeping may endure for a night, But joy comes in the morning. Now in my prosperity I said, "I shall never be moved."

LORD, by Your favor You have made my mountain stand strong; You hid Your face, and I was troubled. I cried out to You, O LORD; And to the LORD I made supplication: "What profit is there in my blood, When I go down to the pit?
Will the dust praise You? Will it declare Your truth? Hear, O LORD, and have mercy on me; LORD, be my helper!" You have turned for me my mourning into dancing; You have put off my sackcloth and clothed me with gladness, To the end that my glory may sing praise to You and not be silent. O LORD my God, I will give thanks to You forever. Psalm 30

Thy navel is like a round goblet, which wanteth not liquor: thy belly is like an heap of wheat set about with lilies. (7:2)
I had the opportunity to travel back to the town where I found the Holy Spirit and host a women's retreat at a wonderful little church high on the mountains above town. I was meditating on my children as I drove. This was their birthday. Although they are 4 years a part, they share the same birthday. I was thinking of how I am so blessed to have them and even though they are grown and the umbilical cord has been long cut, they live deep in my heart. Their navels had been a sign to me of how we were connected to each other. God spoke to me while I was driving and said, "I have chosen the day that you gave birth to your children in the natural, to birth in you something new." Wow isn't God awesome! Only he could arrange something like that. I had grown from a baby in Christ, but yet still so attached to him. He had let me know if he sent me out, he would equip me. I would never lack when I give Him out. One of the first words he spoke directly to me told me this and I did not understand at that time.

"You have been destined from the beginning for great things. You have been destined to teach my people my heart, to touch me, to catch my ear. Fear not, for my favor is upon you."

One of the greatest things on earth is to see a person with a dead defeated spirit, come back to life in Christ.

We so often just want to see a physical resurrection but to me this spiritual resurrection is by far the greatest! I know and understand this as a truth because I have lived through it.

"He who believes in Me, as the Scripture has said, out of his heart will flow rivers of living water." John 7:38

I have the words of eternal life deep within my belly. I have heavenly manna to give to others! So do you! This is the inner beauty that dwells in me and you.

"but whoever drinks of the water that I shall give him will never thirst. But the water that I shall give him will become in him a fountain of water springing up into everlasting life." John 4:14

Thy two breasts are like two young roes that are twins. (7:3)
The balance now in my life is faith and love. He is love but without faith I cannot please him. Before God had only spoken into my life about what I would be. I was becoming what He had said. Now he is telling me that this is a truth for my life now, because others can see it, not just Him. They can see that through trials, I can love but still have the faith that God can move mountains.

Thy neck is as a tower of ivory; thine eyes like the fishpools in Heshbon, by the gate of Bathrabbim: thy nose is as the tower of Lebanon which looketh toward Damascus. (7:4)
My neck or will had changed. There is a costly price for having a strong and rare will to do the right thing for God. There have been many times in my life where doing the right thing cost me things in the physical realm.

Most recently doing the right thing cost me my job during a time of high unemployment. I am not lifting myself up but it would have been much easier to compromise and keep my job. Through all of this, my friends could see a still, deep quiet in my eyes. This was the peace of God, which many cannot understand where this peace came from. No one can take this peace from me, only I can choose to give it up.

Some of the cleanest pools in the land at that time were the pools in Heshbon. Bath Rabbim means the unique daughter among many. He was telling, "I have given you peace so that your life will be unmoved and not polluted by the unrest and turmoil of the world and the people that are around you. You will have clean fresh water for many to drink while other will choose to die of thirst."

When I look at the bridegroom, my eyes now are like the eyes of a dove and watching for His return. When I look at the world, they see the peace in my eyes. This excites me on my walk because it is very easy for all to see peace when I am resting in His presence but for others to see it in the hard times is amazing. Only God can do that!

The nose is for smelling. The tower of Lebanon was a watchtower critical to the protection of Israel. I can now smell or discern the enemy coming as long as my face is turned towards the Lord.

Thine head upon thee is like Carmel, and the hair of thine head like purple; the king is held in the galleries. (7:5)
Mount Carmel is known for being fertile and very fruitful. Carmel means mountain garden. God had a purpose in saving me!

I will not have a small self-centered view of what he has done for me! I am separated from this world for His purposes. Purple also points to royal, but have you ever thought about the fact that is made from two colors, red and blue? I could say this royal color of my separation has come from a combination of suffering and the presence of God. This has caught His attention, somehow I just know this. That is so amazing to me to think that I could catch His eye with the death to my flesh.

How fair and how pleasant art thou, O love, for delights! (7:6)
I can hardly believe what I am hearing in my spirit. These are almost the same words I spoke to Him. Can He really see me as something so wonderful? I am truly being transformed by His love and this is pleasing to Him. To be honest, I feel so unworthy of His assessment because I always seem to focus on my faults. I am realizing that when I focus on my faults, I have taken my eyes off Him. This is giving me great strength to continue this journey, knowing each step I take, no matter how small, is one step closer to His image. This is most pleasing to my King, my bridegroom.

But we all, with unveiled face, beholding as in a mirror the glory of the Lord, are being transformed into the same image from glory to glory, just as by the Spirit of the Lord. 2 Corinthians 3:18

This thy stature is like to a palm tree, and thy breasts to clusters of grapes. (7:7)

If you were out in the desert or should I say a very dry land and off in the distance you saw a tall palm tree; then you would know you are heading in the right direction to getting a cool drink of water. That is where a palm grows naturally.

A palm grows in clusters. It is weak when growing alone but when there are three or four together they strengthen each other. Have you ever seen a bent and crooked palm tree? A palm has incredible resistance to the winds of life. This is how my bridegroom sees me and you! You are a sign leading to the water of life in a dry world; a sign that draws its life not from its surroundings but from a clear deep pool of refreshing water.

The fruit of the palm grows high in the air. The fruit is not accessible for just anyone who passes by; but for those who are willing to climb high to reach it. If the fruit was reachable for anyone to pluck off, it could be devastating for the tree and future growth. Not everyone takes care when they pick fruit. God is showing me this because I believe that the height or should I say the presence of God in my life is what has caused me to bear fruit.

And the Spirit and the bride say, "Come!" And let him who hears say, "Come!" And let him who thirsts come. Whoever desires, let him take the water of life freely. Rev 22:17

I said, I will go up to the palm tree, I will take hold of the boughs thereof: now also thy breasts shall be as clusters of the vine, and the smell of thy nose like apples; (7:8)
This is a promise from the bridegroom for me and you. As He takes hold of my life and speaks into it, the fruit of my life that has grown in His presence is now like new wine to others. Others are seeing that what God has done for me. He can do the same for them also.

They can see that while looking at me, that their lives do not have to be like a desert with no water and they do not have to be fruitless, with no power or beauty. God has no favorites in life. It is the life I have chosen which is living near to the bridegroom that is attractive.

They, too, will also find support in the climb as I did. It is not that I am the source of food and drink but He who dwells inside of me is the source of life.

In the second chapter, the bridegroom is described as like the apple tree in the forest. Now He is telling me the sweetness of my breath is the result of feeding off this apple tree in the forest. Breath is what makes a man live. Can you see that He is speaking into my life, that every single breath, every breath I exhale is the fragrance of Christ dwelling deep within my heart? That is a promise I cherish!

How sweet are Your words to my taste, Sweeter than honey to my mouth! Psalm 119:103

And the roof of thy mouth like the best wine for my beloved, that goeth down sweetly, causing the lips of those that are asleep to speak. (7:9)
Once more He kisses me. He has smelled my breathe and kisses me so He can taste what is in my mouth. This is the most intimate kiss yet. He is restoring to my mind so many things that been beaten down over the years. Now I can see I am chosen! It has brought revival to my spirit. I can feel His power rising up with me. This is the beginning of the manifestation of His glory in me; His love is beginning to pour out of me.

"So the last will be first, and the first last. For many are called, but few chosen." Matt 20:16

And he said to him, "Every man at the beginning sets out the good wine, and when the guests have well drunk, then the inferior. You have kept the good wine until now!" John 2:10

For all the promises of God in Him are Yes, and in Him Amen, to the glory of God through us. 2 Cor 1:20

The wine of bridal love is the ultimate in wines! There is no fermenting in it. I have entered into the place where God has taken ahold of my words. I speak for Him. My words have become full of His love and His will yet seasoned with salt. My own words are becoming fewer. I am still working on controlling my own words from coming out but it is all a process. As Christians, we sometimes speak words of love, yet forget the salt that is needed. Allowing God to take control of your words is the easiest way to accomplish this. I know that on my own I cannot do it. I have sometimes spoken things out of God's timing and wished I could take the words back. We can be too quick to want to share everything we know. When I allow God to have my words, life comes forth to awaken those that were sleeping.

I am my beloved's, and his desire is toward me. (7:10)
This is a new declaration for me. I now understand that we are one. I have given myself to Him forever. I do not possess Him and it is not what He does for me that moves my heart; it is the fact that we are one. He is the air I breathe, my every heartbeat and always on my mind. I now can see how much He desires me. Me! It is so strange to see it and even believe it after all the rejection that I lived through, but I know that His desire is toward me!

Come, my beloved, let us go forth into the field; let us lodge in the villages. (7:11)

I had always been very recluse most of my life. I didn't like to go out and about, but stay in my safe and secure places. Something has so changed in me. All of the sudden I want to take my Lord out with me into the villages. This is not a place that I will take a short visit to and then retreat back into myself; but a place I plan to stay at with Him.

In the spirit we dwell together, we are one. I want to go out and share what He has done for me. He no longer has to draw me. He desires me just as I am and now I can see the purpose I was created for. I cannot do this alone but with Him all things are possible, even for me. That was a new concept for me, yet it flows so freely from my heart now. Where ever he takes me, we are at home together.

For if we have been united together in the likeness of His death, certainly we also shall be in the likeness of His resurrection, knowing this, that our old man was crucified with Him, that the body of sin might be done away with, that we should no longer be slaves of sin. Romans 6:5-6

I will have Him go with me, even though deep inside I know it means I will experience more trials and more shaping of my character. I know I still harbor deep hurts that need to come out in His timing but I do not care! Together we will deal with whatever comes up. I love Him so much! I have never been intimate with anyone on this level and cannot image living a moment without him.

Let us get up early to the vineyards; let us see if the vine flourish, whether the tender grape appear, and the pomegranates bud forth: there will I give thee my loves. (7:12)

This seems to have a two-fold meaning for me. I want to find out if all the things I know he has done in my life are flourishing. I am willing to allow him to search my heart to find the things that are so well hidden that only He can find them. I will give Him my love by allowing Him to search and heal those things that are deep in my soul. I know this will be painful but I love Him so much that it is not a concern to me anymore.

I am willing to put aside my earthly rest to go out with Him to see what is happening in the church and beyond with the lost people of this world. I will give Him my love here by doing what He directs me to do. I will share of His love and healing power. Salvation of the lost and the backslidden are heavy on my heart. I must remember that a blossom is only a promise of fruit. The plant must be watered and nourished before it can bear fruit. I will not let the blossom grow in vain. A blossom leaves a reminder of a fragrance and will eventually be a mess on the ground when the winds blow on it. Without continued nurturing there will be not be fruit for the benefit of both God and us. We must bear fruit for His glory.

The mandrakes give a smell, and at our gates are all manner of pleasant fruits, new and old, which I have laid up for thee, O my beloved. (7:13)
A mandrake is called a love apple. It is purple in color. All the suffering I have experience combined with the presence of God give off a fragrance of love. The suffering here means dying to myself and letting go of the things that need to go. I will not allow the fruit in my life to go bad. I will press into this intimacy deeper and He will preserve me; all for His glory. I will not keep my eyes on the fruit with pride but I will keep my eyes on the one who preserves me. My treasures are laid up in Heaven not here on this earth. This is what I give Him in love.

"Do not lay up for yourselves treasures on earth, where moth and rust destroy and where thieves break in and steal; but lay up for yourselves treasures in heaven, where neither moth nor rust destroys and where thieves do not break in and steal." Matt 6:19-20

Chapter 9
Leaning On My Beloved

O that thou wert as my brother, that sucked the breasts of my mother! when I should find thee without, I would kiss thee; yea, I should not be despised. (8:1)
I have never been one to make a scene in public. It seems at times so confusing when you love the Lord, to figure out what is proper and what is not. I see people who let their emotions control their actions. Some being hyper-spiritual seemed to think that this would show their great love; others hide their spirituality in the walls of the church building. At time the Song was written, it was not proper to kiss except an immediate family member in public such as a brother or sister. Men and women were forbidden to kiss in public.

"I love you so much, my bridegroom! Please show me the balance here!" I cried out. He gave me just one word, "Relationship". A bride has the right to kiss her husband in public. I believe He was telling me if I walked as His bride; then I had the right and no one would despise me for it. "I do not want to look like I am proud about my love Lord. I just love you so much!" Then He gave me a very firm word, "You have to keep your eyes on me!"

I thought and thought about this reply I had been given. I thought about all I had suffered in my life because of the opinions and stabbing words of others. Then I thought of how this love I had found had broken though all the walls of protection I had built. Sudden I knew the truth and shouted out, "I love you all the time, not just when we are hidden." I had gone beyond the point of caring what others thought about this love I had found, even those outside the church. The lesson here is to determine what is kissing the Lord in public. I would say it is not some display of a physical touch but a willingness to do his will, no matter what.

I would lead thee, and bring thee into my mother's house, who would instruct me: I would cause thee to drink of spiced wine of the juice of my pomegranate. (8:2)

I want to share my Bridegroom with others. I want to usher in the presence of God for all who enter His house. I do not think that a lot of Christians understand the power of the presence of God. They do not understand that in His presence is the greatest healing for the soul, peace beyond understanding and joy unspeakable. The presence of God is real!! The presence is not a figure of speech or a Christian term. I am not content to share His love with just those I work with. I have to bring His presence back into the church! I think some of the most hurting people in the world are within the walls of the church. They put up walls in fear of what others would think of them and their need. I want them to experience what I have! I want them to live up the potential God has placed inside of them! How are we to win the world if His presence is not within our houses of worship so we can go to receive refreshment to continue on?

I got saved in a church where the presence was so evident that people traveled hundreds of miles to come to church. I could not believe that something so wonderful was not welcomed in so many of God's houses. Why do they call them God's house if His presence is not allowed in? I was actually surprised and sad to find that all churches were not like mine.

The best wines were ones mixed with spices. I wanted to give Him my best. It is really amazing when you see the purpose in your life. I may not be a bible scholar but I know the deepness of the presence of God. I am healed in the presence of a Holy God. I yearn for my brothers and sisters to know this presence.

I am working on knowing the word. I have discovered if I spend time in His presence and then study the word, it comes alive! This works for me but maybe the reverse would work for you. I just know the importance of the presence of God in my life. The best of me is brought out and the worst of me dies in His presence.

Lift up your heads, O you gates! Lift up, you everlasting doors! And the King of glory shall come in. Psalm 24:9

Juice is made by pressing or squeezing the fruit to remove the juice. All hardness is taken away. Are you willing to give Jesus the juice of your life? One thing I know for sure; this process is much easier to accomplish if you spend time in His presence.

His left hand should be under my head, and his right hand should embrace me. I charge you, O daughters of Jerusalem, that ye stir not up, nor awake my love, until he please. (8:3-4) He supports my thoughts and embraces me to a deeper depth than before. I know that my experiences with Him in the physical may never be what they were before. I have matured past that point in my life but would welcome the experience again with open arms. Now there is a relationship much deeper in my spirit, where before it was much more on the surface or physical. I had needed to experience his touch again and again in the physical to compensate for the empty hole left by my childhood. I am healed of that need now and can go onto a deeper relationship with Him. Yes, the physical is awesome and comes from time to time now but it does not sustain me. The deep spiritual relationship is what keeps me going.

It is as if a door to an eternal relationship has opened and I have walked through it. If He would never touch me again in the physical, the relationship I have now is enough. I know the choice of when His love comes is completely up to Him. When His purpose for my life becomes fruitful, it will be in His timing. He knows my needs and I will walk in the faith that He will always be there for me.

Who is this that cometh up from the wilderness, leaning upon her beloved? I raised thee up under the apple tree: there thy mother brought thee forth: there she brought thee forth that bare thee. (8:5)
It is so much fun to meet people I have not seen for many years. From time to time I run into people who knew me in my former sinful life and they are amazed by the change and my commitment and love for God. It is a great opportunity to share of the love I have found. I have truly come out of the wilderness leaning on my beloved. Some are happy with the change, others run away as fast as they can. I just pray blessings that they can find what I have and understand the joy I have.

To the one we are the aroma of death leading to death, and to the other the aroma of life leading to life. And who is sufficient for these things? 2 Cor 2:16

I will never forget the moment that God awakened my heart and the ones in the church who loved me unconditionally. I was loved just as I was. My life was not changed through worldly counseling but by the presence of God and with those precious ones working as His hands and mouth to nurture me to spiritual health. I had two precious Christian counselors I talked with but that was so different from worldly counseling.

I found life when I found Him. Sometimes He takes me back in the spirit to that wonderful time. It was wonderful yet so painful to die to my flesh. Anytime I go back, it always has a purpose for good.

Set me as a seal upon thine heart, as a seal upon thine arm: for love is strong as death; jealousy is cruel as the grave: the coals thereof are coals of fire, which hath a most vehement flame. (8:6)
If you can reach this point in your walk, I would say you are sold out. Since I knew that I would not necessarily experience that physical touch for a while, I cried out to Him, "Never let me lose the place I have in your heart, my lover, my king! No matter what happens from here until you come for me; let me always be close to you!" I knew if I was always on His heart, I would have the mercy and grace I need to complete my earthly destiny. If my name is upon His arm, His power and strength is mine. I know that He has promised to do the same for me. He will set his seal upon me. I need to continue to press on for His glory.

"He who overcomes, I will make him a pillar in the temple of My God, and he shall go out no more. I will write on him the name of My God and the name of the city of My God, the New Jerusalem, which comes down out of heaven from My God. And I will write on him My new name." Rev 3:12

I can now understand the emotions of divine love. It is the strongest thing I have ever experienced. I cannot hide it or keep it under the control of my walls. For me He died and chose death so I might live.

"Greater love has no one than this, than to lay down one's life for his friends." John 15:13

I have decided that now that I will lay down my life for my friends and friends to be. Not so much as to die in the physical, but to die to my flesh and reflect Jesus as much as I can. Many people I know give more to their friends than they do Jesus. I cannot walk that path. All I have to give my friends is the Jesus in me. My heart burns with a violently passionate fire for my bridegroom. He is always on my mind and heart. If you walk around my home, you will find his picture everywhere. He is that important to me! The more I die the more the flame in my heart burns. I know that the Lord is jealous of anything that takes my attention from Him. He sees my burning heart and it pleases Him.

For I am jealous for you with godly jealousy. For I have betrothed you to one husband, that I may present you as a chaste virgin to Christ. 2 Cor 11:2

Many waters cannot quench love, neither can the floods drown it: if a man would give all the substance of his house for love, it would utterly be contemned. (8:7)
To this point I have learned that His love is truly a banner of victory over me. His love covers me and never fails me. My friends and family can fail me but His love is always there! I may not always agree in my flesh with His choices but I understand tough love and know He only wants the best for me. It does not matter what obstacles in life face me, His love is covering me and helping me to overcome. He protects me and I know it.

So shall they fear the name of the LORD from the west, and his glory from the rising of the sun. When the enemy shall come in like a flood, the Spirit of the LORD shall lift up a standard against him. Isaiah 59:19

My family could not understand why when God began moving in our lives we sold our home and moved to a little town in the middle of nowhere. We felt strongly God was urging us to go. We had no jobs or even prospects of one. The county we were moving to had one of, if not the highest, unemployment rate in the state. My husband always joked that it was truly God's country because you couldn't make it without him. We sold the house, cashed in our retirement and headed for our destiny. We rolled into town with $75,000 and left with nothing. We spent it all living there to survive. The tradeoff is that we found...the Holy Spirit and I got saved!

If you talked to some, they would tell you it was the worst possible financial decision we could have made. My husband had a good job and we had a large home in one of the nicest neighborhoods in town near the river. It looked like we were living the American dream but something was lacking in our lives. What would you pay to have your life change and find love? We have no retirement now and have a larger mortgage than we have ever had. My house is small and needs work but I have never been happier. It was the best money I have ever spent and worth every penny!

This scripture is not only talking about your wealth but I think also about your flesh. We think too much of ourselves. We would like to keep our pride and self-righteousness. What would you give up to gain everything?

Yet indeed I also count all things loss for the excellence of the knowledge of Christ Jesus my Lord, for whom I have suffered the loss of all things, and count them as rubbish, that I may gain Christ and be found in Him, not having my own righteousness, which is from the law, but that which is through faith in Christ, the righteousness which is from God by faith; that I may know Him and the power of His resurrection, and the fellowship of His sufferings, being conformed to His death, if, by any means, I may attain to the resurrection from the dead. Phil 3:8-11

It is all a process that none of us will complete until we meet Him face to face in Heaven. We need to encourage each other to press on.

Not that I have already attained, or am already perfected; but I press on, that I may lay hold of that for which Christ Jesus has also laid hold of me. Phil 3:12

We have a little sister, and she hath no breasts: what shall we do for our sister in the day when she shall be spoken for? (8:8)
Something changed in my mind once I realized that we are all spoken for. Jesus wants all of us to be His bride, no matter what type of person you are. It became more personal to share the gospel.
If my neighbor's child was missing, my heart would go out to them and I would try to help. If my child was missing, it would become a more personal pursuit to find the child. So it is the same with the lost in the world. If you can see in your heart that they are part of your family in Christ and they have not yet chosen to enter into that place yet, then your heart changes.

It also became more personal to help equip those in the church who are immature. I have found a family beyond my biological family that just keeps growing. There are ones that are not crying out for His kisses and do not understand His covering of love for them yet. I can see that I have a responsibility to help bring them up. I can partner with Jesus to help in this task as he directs me.

"For whoever does the will of My Father in heaven is My brother and sister and mother." Matt 12:50

"Sing, O barren, You who have not borne! Break forth into singing, and cry aloud, You who have not labored with child! For more are the children of the desolate Than the children of the married woman," says the LORD. Isaiah 54:1

If she be a wall, we will build upon her a palace of silver: and if she be a door, we will inclose her with boards of cedar. (8:9)
I can see that these dear sisters must become a wall of strength for Him and a door for others to enter in. She must learn to be truly committed to Him. I know that her growth can only come through the Lord but I can be his hands and mouth, if I listen. I can help her to find many of the truths the Lord has for her life. I will pray to the Lord for help and protection over her as she grows.
A Song of Ascents. Of Solomon. Unless the LORD builds the house, They labor in vain who build it; Unless the LORD guards the city, The watchman stays awake in vain. Psalm 127:1

I have grown so much in the Lord since I found the Holy Spirit. I know that when the Lord begins a work, He will finish it. I am blessed to be a part no matter how small. She must become a habitation for the King! I can teach her the truths I have found in my pursuit.

Having been built on the foundation of the apostles and prophets, Jesus Christ Himself being the chief cornerstone, in whom the whole building, being fitted together, grows into a holy temple in the Lord, in whom you also are being built together for a dwelling place of God in the Spirit. Eph 2:20-22

I am a wall, and my breasts like towers: then was I in his eyes as one that found favour. (8:10)

I am a wall. The fiery darts of the enemy seem to bounce off me. When I need help in my journey the Lord is quick to direct me. He sends my friends when I am beginning to get down with the life that surrounds me. He gives me words to uplift my spirit. I am not a super Christian; I just know where to turn for help. He never promised me that this would be an easy path to walk. I just know what awaits me at the end.

I have found the balance of faith and love in my life. I am pressing on to reach the point in my life that I can continually walk in the place of balance. Sometimes I lose my balance but am quick to recover now. I have an authority in Him; this allows me to give freely of myself to others. I am getting closer to my destiny and I believe there is a peace in my eyes that has never existed before. I am the Shulamite, the daughter of peace.

Solomon had a vineyard at Baalhamon; he let out the vineyard unto keepers; every one for the fruit thereof was to bring a thousand pieces of silver. (8:11)
Baal Hamon literally means lord or possessor of abundance. The Lord has given me a vineyard to tend. I am responsible to help nurture God's people to maturity and I must give an accounting in the end of what I have done.

"Therefore you also be ready, for the Son of Man is coming at an hour you do not expect. Who then is a faithful and wise servant, whom his master made ruler over his household, to give them food in due season? Blessed is that servant whom his master, when he comes, will find so doing. Matt 24:44-46

I do not know the time He is coming back, so I must continue to put my life behind me and continue working for Him. I work a full time job so I know the excuses that come with that. I am always wishing I could do more but I do what I can.

I figure if God wants me to minister full time then He will free my time. In the mean time I see a vineyard that needs tending at my workplace, in the stores and all the places my life takes me. You never know what one kind word will sow into someone's spirit. The important thing is to do what you are supposed to do.

My vineyard, which is mine, is before me: thou, O Solomon, must have a thousand, and those that keep the fruit thereof two hundred (8:12)
I can now look at myself and say, "Lord, I understand that my life is mine to give. I am responsible for me. Others have helped along the way and may you bless them with a double portion. I give myself to you for your purposes, to bear fruit for your glory. I will continue to rest in your presence and study your word so that I may fulfill my destiny."

This is so different from when I first began. I know that I must guard my heart, not to put up walls to keep everything out but to only allow goods things to enter. This will save me a lot of trouble and pain on this journey.

Keep your heart with all diligence, For out of it spring the issues of life. Prov 4:23

Thou that dwellest in the gardens, the companions hearken to thy voice: cause me to hear it. (8:13)
The Lord loves to hear my voice and yours! I love to pray and worship Him. To me worship is an intimate conversation between Him and me. That is the way I work and He loves it because He made me.

I now cry out, "Lord, those around me also want to hear your voice and I know you want to hear theirs. Give me the words to speak to them to help them enter that intimate place of fellowship." It is not about me anymore. I am happy with my life and the only thing I want is to get closer to Him.

Make haste, my beloved, and be thou like to a roe or to a young hart upon the mountains of spices. (8:14)
Although I am happy with my life there is a deep burning and dissatisfaction in me that will never go away until He returns for me and you, His bride. He has brought me so far on this journey and I do not know what is next but I will continue to do His will.

Therefore be patient, brethren, until the coming of the Lord. See how the farmer waits for the precious fruit of the earth, waiting patiently for it until it receives the early and latter rain. You also be patient. Establish your hearts, for the coming of the Lord is at hand. James 5:7-8

Sometimes I feel on top of the world other times I feel like Job but I continue on. Even through all the trials of life and things that do not seem fair, I know in the end we will meet face to face and that is the desire of my heart.

And after my skin is destroyed, this I know, That in my flesh I shall see God, Whom I shall see for myself, And my eyes shall behold, and not another. How my heart yearns within me! Job 19:26-27

The Lord understands my desires but I also know everything in my life is in His timing. I see such a limited picture of life and the spirit. Until He comes I will not be as a well dammed up or a light under a basket. I will give freely to all who come with an open heart to know my King.

And the Spirit and the bride say, "Come!" And let him who hears say, "Come!" And let him who thirsts come. Whoever desires, let him take the water of life freely. Rev 22:17

"May God be your strength and covering on your journey, a banner of love flying high over your life. May the greatest love song ever sung become a reality in your heart. It was written just for you and I pray that Jesus will become your Songs of Songs forever and ever. I bless you my sisters and brothers on your path to your destiny."